Note: Just as this book was going to press I learned of the sad death of my great friend and collaborator Derek Cross, so many of whose photographs adorn the pages of this book. His vivid personality and his artistry will much be missed, and the field day we had together at Carnforth at the time he secured the picture on the dust jacket will always be a cherished memory.

O. S. Nock

FROM THE FOOTPLATE

FROM THE FOOTPLATE

REMINISCENCES OF THE LAST YEARS OF STEAM

O. S. NOCK

B Sc, C Eng, F I C E, F I Mech E

Past President and Honorary Fellow,
Institution of Railway Signal Engineers

GUILD PUBLISHING
LONDON

This edition published 1984 by
Book Club Associates
By arrangement with Granada Publishing Limited

Copyright © O. S. Nock 1984

Printed in Great Britain by
William Collins Sons & Co Ltd, Great Britain

CONTENTS

PREFACE

It is appropriate that these reminiscences of mine, of the latter days of steam on the British railways, should have the collective title *From the Footplate* because in taking a backward look to 1934, when I first had the privilege of riding in the driver's cab of an express locomotive, one's attitude towards steam locomotives, their attributes and no less their weaknesses, tended to stem from practical experience of their behaviour in traffic. I carry with me always the most vivid memories of the men who drove and fired these great machines, and of the many facets of human nature that those journeys invoked. All my rides on the footplate were officially authorized, in some cases by the Chief Mechanical Engineers of the railways concerned. But the magic card of authority was no infallible welcome in the driver's cab; there it was personalities that counted, though in the nigh-fifty years that I have enjoyed this privilege I can recall only one occasion – and then not on a steam locomotive – when I was not made welcome. I recall with a relish the occasion when I had joined the London–Aberdeen Postal special at Carlisle, around the witching hour, done a good deal of notetaking in the travelling post-office vans, and then soon after dawn presented my engine-pass to the driver at Stirling. When I made to stow myself in the right-hand corner of the cab, out of the way, he exclaimed: 'Och, if ye're on here ye're the dr-r-r-iver.' And I drove the Postal from Sterling to Perth!

There is, however, a deeper significance to these memories of mine. The end of the steam era on the railways of Britain was a time of historical significance far transcending a mere change in the form of motive power. It marked the culmination, perhaps a little prematurely, of one of the greatest developments the world has ever known. It is important in that its influence was constructional rather than destructional. It is a sobering thought to try and imagine how 19th-century history might have run if the steam locomotive had not been made to go; if there had been no steam railways to link up the growing industrial areas of Great Britain, to support the colonization of Canada and to facilitate the development of the United States; to become the 'right hand' of Cecil Rhodes in the evolution of southern Africa. We are, however, too near the official end of steam traction on the railways of Great Britain – the autumn of 1968 – for a fully definitive assessment of the part it played in national and indeed world history. Partisan feelings still tend to run high, and the resulting evocation clouds the coldly dispassionate analysis of bed-rock fundamentals that are so essential to any true appraisal of the facts as they become known.

Nor are the facts themselves established in their

entirety, yet. Among the vast proliferation of modern books there are countless biographies and autobiographies of famous and less famous people, and in recent years not a few of these have been about railwaymen. Some of those who became leading actors in the drama of railway nationalization in Britain have themselves contributed to this modern trend. When the axe began to fall enthusiasts by the hundred flocked to the linesides, with cameras, cines and tape recorders; and with a professionalism for which one can have nothing but unbounded admiration they documented the last regular workings of every remaining steam locomotive design. The fact that, as time went on, and the end drew ever nearer, the majority of steam locomotives had degenerated into a state of filth that our forebears would have found beyond belief did not matter. The documentation was faithful, and vitally important for future historians.

The results are to be seen in innumerable albums, themselves superb examples of the photographic art. To those of us older in years, however, and like myself with a long professional association with railways, not only in Great Britain but in lands far overseas, the ending of the steam era on British Railways evoked a host of memories of a different kind, linking the events of the last few years with happenings of half a century ago and with men who were the very embodiment of the spirit of the old steam railways. So, in these pages the 'last years' of steam have been interpreted rather liberally.

My thanks are due to the steam locomotive men of every estate who have always made me so welcome in their drawing offices, works and running sheds, and on the footplate, from chief mechanical engineers to the humble cleaner who turned out on a busy Saturday to fire a fast express. Collectively they were a race apart, of whom the memory should remain evergreen.

O. S. Nock
November 1983

CHAPTER 1

THE 'SOU' WEST'

To readers of railway literature in the early 1900s the Glasgow and South Western must have been among the least known, and certainly the least glamourized, of the larger railways of Great Britain. Of the Scottish companies its interest, prestige and fame were eclipsed by the Caledonian, the North British and the Highland, and when the time of the Diamond Jubilee of its incorporation as a company came in October 1910 it was not until six months later that *The Railway Magazine* came up with a group of rather stodgy short articles, clearly strung together from official statistics. *The Railway Magazine* was then at the height of its pre-war opulence, with 88 pages and a colour plate every month all for sixpence(!), and the 27 pages of rather dull stuff allocated to the G & S W R were completely overshadowed in interest by the delightful variety of the rest of the magazine. Furthermore, when I first went to Scotland, about the time of the Grouping, and saw trains of the G & S W R at Carlisle and on the Clyde Coast lines at Paisley, the few locomotives looked dingy and not well cared for. I did not see any of the huge 'Baltic' tanks introduced by Robert Whitelegg.

My first professional contact with the line, albeit no more than a slight one, came early in 1926 not long after I had begun my work as a graduate trainee with the Westinghouse Brake and Saxby

Signal Co., as it then was. During the civil war in Ireland much damage had been done to railway installations and, to avoid the need for replacing signal boxes that had been destroyed, the idea had been conceived of operating remote junction layouts by electrical power from hand generators, at 100 volts. The scheme was patented, and it was arranged that Westinghouse should develop it and furnish the necessary apparatus. Several simple installations had been successfully made, and I had to design the circuits for an interesting case myself, on the Dublin–Cork main line south of Mallow, as part of the rehabilitation work following the destruction of the big viaduct over the River Blackwater. Just to the south of the viaduct was Killarney Junction, where the single-line branch to the west began, and this was redesigned for hand-generator operation from Mallow. Then the Scottish Division of the L M S came up with the idea of operating Challoch Junction in a similar way, from Dunragit.

This lonely outpost was where the G & S W R line southwards from Ayr joined the Portpatrick and Wigtownshire Joint Railway, which came across Galloway westwards from Dumfries. Both routes joining at Challoch Junction were single-tracked, and at first it seemed that the principles developed in Ireland could be readily adapted. But until the project arose I must admit I had never heard of Challoch Junction; it could have been as much 'out in the sticks' as some of the remote places we had re-equipped on the devastated railways of Southern Ireland.

The signal box at Challoch Junction was still in full commission. It was a token exchanging point both on the joint line to Dumfries and on the line up to Girvan, and to eliminate it would have involved single-line token working between Dunragit and Glenluce, in the first case, and between Dunragit and New Luce in the second, distances of 3.4 and 6.7 miles respectively. Issue of the appropriate tokens would have to have been interlocked with the lie of the points at Challoch Junction, as we had done at Banagher Junction in Ireland, from a hand generator installation at

Clara. The trouble was, however, that at Challoch Junction there was a loop road on the line northward to Ayr, which the L M S wished to retain. The section northward to New Luce was heavily graded and 5½ miles long, often taking the best part of 15 minutes to clear, and they wanted to be able to cross northbound and southbound trains at Challoch Junction. As a mere junior I remember pointing out that it was far from a simple case of token interlocking, and I heard no more about it

---

Currock shed, Carlisle: G & S W R engines, left to right: a Manson 4–6–0, believed to be No. 496; Manson large-boilered 4–4–0, and two Drummond express goods 2–6–0s   *Courtesy David L. Smith*

14

until four years later, and then in no more than a roundabout way. Apparently a group of senior Westinghouse engineers had subsequently got together and produced a scheme for Challoch Junction. We then had a northern representative, resident at Leeds, who dealt with everything north of the Trent, and he was briefed to put the scheme up to Scottish Region; it was in 1930 when I was working on site at Glasgow St Enoch that I learned of the fate of the Challoch Junction proposals, when I was in close touch with men who were then in what might be termed the middle strata of engineering management.

In pre-Grouping days the men of the Glasgow and South Western had always been on cat and dog terms with their opposite numbers of the Caledonian; and when the government Grouping scheme of 1923 brought both these Scottish companies into the L M S system, with ultimate headquarters in London, the old rivalries continued even though there was some fusion of staff. In the signal and telegraph department the new chief in Scotland was a Caledonian man, but all those in authority at St Enoch were ex-G & S W, and they completely disregarded not only their new boss over at Buchanan Street, but headquarters in London as well! They were a tough lot, those men of the Sou' West, but extraordinarily likeable and

One of R. Whitelegg's huge 4–6–4 tanks on a local coast train near Troon

grand to work with. They were sons and grandsons of men who had fought the Caledonian all their lives, and when the L M S appointed as Chief Engineer a man who had formerly been on the Highland their disdain was considerable. We in Westinghouse had suffered from his rather stiff-necked attitude to our problems when we were resignalling Victoria and Exchange stations in Manchester, and when a similar situation over the point blades arose at St Enoch we told one of the senior permanent way men of our experience. His reply was terse: 'Och, dinna' fash yersel'; Euston's a long way awa'!'

I shall always remember an incident, slight in itself, but which emphasized the happy way in which I was accepted into their circle. I went north with two senior Westinghouse engineers and at a full dress meeting in the main offices in Glasgow I was introduced as a draughtsman. Arrangements were made for me to work in a wooden hut on the outer end of one of the platforms at St Enoch, where a drawing board, tee-square and other implements were to be made available. Then we went on site and I met the men with whom I had to work in the ensuing days. My function was explained to them and in the course of the introductions Willie Brown, the electrical assistant, looked at me with a twinkle in his eye and in a loud stage whisper said to old Fred Flint, then 'our man in Glasgow' and a great personal friend of mine, 'He looks quite respectable!'

One of those I met at St Enoch, and who rejoiced in their relative immunity from interference by headquarters, was Johnny Melville, the District Engineer, son of a rather formidable character who had been Engineer-in-Chief of the Glasgow and South Western from 1891 to 1916, and who, I was told, went by the homely nickname of 'Bloody Bill'. His son I found to be a cheerful, light-hearted character, but in view of his one-time aversion to anything on the English side of the L M S I was amused when he was brought to London, as permanent way engineer of the whole system. At St Enoch I had met and enjoyed the company of men in the middle strata of engineering responsibility,

and I had realized that a great spirit lingered in those who had served the Glasgow and South Western Railway. In January 1939 from the pages of *The Railway Magazine* I began to learn still more.

In three successive Januarys, leading into the darkest days of the Second World War, the eagerly awaited Special Scottish Number of *The Railway Magazine* was enlivened by an article by David L. Smith, of Ayr: 'G & S W Nights' Entertainments'; 'More G & S W Nights' Entertainments'; and 'Still More G & S W Nights' Entertainments'. Of the episodes he recalled some were vivid, some hilarious, but all revealed a profound knowledge of railway engineering and operation. There is no doubt, however, that amid the enjoyment with which these articles were received there were not a few readers, particularly south of the Border, who regarded some of the events he described as slightly apocryphal. But I had corresponded with Davie Smith on several occasions, and when business in Scotland in the early months of 1945 left me with a free Sunday I went down to Ayr and spent a day with him and his father. My first impression was of surprise, that a teller of such soul-stirring adventures on the footplate should be a slender, almost frail, scholarly man passing beyond middle age. He was quiet, shy in his demeanour and precise of speech, but with a personality revealed by a twinkle in the eye; and his conversation was enriched by the frequent flashes of humour that permeated his articles. I came to appreciate too, however, that of the stories he told so brilliantly in *The Railway Magazine*, he had taken the greatest care to check all the facts before committing them to paper.

The memory, atmosphere and spirit of the Glasgow and South Western Railway lingered long in south-west Scotland – long after the railway itself had been absorbed into the L M S. I had met it first, head on, in 1930 when I went to Glasgow on behalf of Westinghouse and I met it again in stirring circumstances on a wild January night in 1949, when I had an engine pass to ride the 'Glesca' Paddy' up from Stranraer. I have the

At Ayr, in the last L M S days: David L. Smith, centre, with the driver and fireman of a 2–6–4 tank engine No. 2277 before leaving for Glasgow

O. S. Nock

reputation of being a good sailor, but I certainly needed all my strength of stomach in the crossing from Larne that night, particularly as I had a privileged place on the navigating bridge of the ship, and was particularly well placed to feel the full effects of the gale. But I thoroughly enjoyed it all, not least the amusement of my nautical friends when during the last stages of the crossing I was climbing into overalls ready to ride on the engine of the boat train. Even in the confines of Loch Ryan the wind was roaring up from the sea, and when I changed over from ship to train the cab of the locomotive was distinctly air conditioned. The engine was one of the ubiquitous Stanier 'Black Five' 4–6–0s, with a splendid pair of men in driver James Stroyan and fireman Archie McGhee.

The wind screamed round the engine as we started away from the pier, crossed the open causeway and had a last sight of the ship and the harbour lights; then away for Dunragit, of signal-ling memories for me, and the leftward turn at Challoch Junction to begin the great climb over the Chirmorie. It is true that we had a load of only four bogie corridor coaches but on such a road, and on such a night, no load can be considered a trifle. Through New Luce; out over the viaduct, and then on to the dreaded length of 1 in 57 ascent. As we forged our way up over the moorland a brilliant moon shone out through the flying clouds, and with the engine's exhaust cracking like a pneumatic riveter the speed was gradually falling till we neared the 'Swan's Neck', that great reverse curve right on the heaviest part of the gradient where many a noble engine has been overpowered by its load, and stalled. But our 'Black Five' had things very much in hand and speed was finely held at 33–4 mph till the very last pitch, where there was a momentary drop to 32. Over the crest, out on the high open moor, an orange light shone in the darkness – Glenwhilly distant signal, on; a long slowing, and then a crawl up to a stop in the station. McGhee went to the signal box and learned that a cattle special from Dunragit to Glasgow was ahead of us, and we had to wait until she had cleared the long section to Barrhill. There was no side-tracking her there either. This single-tracked route was busy at this hour of the night, and we learned that at Barrhill the 7.35 p.m. milk empties from Glasgow to Stranraer was waiting in the loop.

To those who did not know the old steam railways, that long wait for 'line clear', sitting out there in the very back of beyond, might be imagined as something of a bore; but that was not to know that magic atmosphere summed up by the American term 'on the railroad'. The cab of an engine in steam, no less than the personalities of its driver and fireman, has a character of its own, especially at night; and while we waited there, at the lone windy little station of Glenwhilly, listening to the alternate soughing and screeching of the gale and the engine emitting that deep hum that tells of an open blower, the nine minutes we were held passed quickly enough. Then we heard the welcome 'ting-ting' of the block-bell in the signal box, and a moment later the signalman came across with the tablet, our authority to proceed to Barrhill. Climbing again, though on easier gradients in this wild and inhospitable countryside where, more so than anywhere else, enginemen have to 'know' the road, especially at night – because there are no signals, no lineside marks, except the succession of small culverts by which the railway crosses and recrosses the brawling Water of Luce. We were climbing the 1 in 100 gradient at 50 mph and then at last there was a light, not on the railway but far away to the left over the moor, the shepherd's house of Ardnamoil, which told us we were near the Chirmorie Summit, 685 ft above sea-level.

Over the crest, downhill we went, snow fences on both sides of the line, glimpsed in a fleeting gleam of moonlight. Then there was another orange light, Barrhill distant signal; the cattle special was still not out of our way. Another wait of $4\frac{1}{2}$ minutes, and then cautiously down the steep and winding descent to Pinwherry. If it were gradients alone here we could have done the 'ton', but not round those curves! However, when we sighted Pinwherry 'distant' it was clear. The cattle special had been shunted for us, and we made to run through the station at maximum permissible speed. To facilitate the exchanging of single-line tablets at speed this line, like many others in Scotland, is equipped with apparatus for mechanical exchanging. It differed from that most commonly used elsewhere, in being suitable also for engines running tender first. It was designed specially for G & S W R conditions by W. Bryson, father of one of the engineers with whom I worked at St Enoch in 1930. Running through Pinwherry at about 35 mph we delivered the Barrhill tablet, but failed to collect the fresh one. Brakes hard on; stop! McGhee, torch in hand, jumped down and ran back. Tablets have been lost in such circumstances, notably in one case I remember when the pouch rolled down a steep embankment and fell into a canal; but in two minutes he was back again in the cab with the pouch and its precious disc, and away we started up the very steep bank to Pinmore.

We were soon making good time again, but because of the stops at Glenwhilly and Barrhill and the unforeseen delay at Pinwherry, we were now running 10 minutes late; but having passed through the summit tunnel and begun the precipice-like descent to Girvan, on a gradient of 1 in 54, speed had to be severely restrained. Nearing the coast there opens up one of the greatest sights to be seen from a train anywhere in the British Isles, the great rock of Ailsa Craig rising to more than 1100 ft, sheer out of the Firth of Clyde some 10 miles out from the shore. I had hoped that the low, rain-laden clouds that were flying in on the wings of this intense cyclone might part for a moment, and that a fitful moon might give us a momentary glimpse of the crag; but instead we eased our way down into Girvan in the teeth of a terrific squall. While we stood, taking water, the wind flung the side doors of the cab open as if they were canvas; the rain lashed the engine and tender as if shot from a hose, and below us in the deserted streets of Girvan the water ran like a river.

'Right away'! Double line now, and every chance of a clear run to Ayr; we were still nearly nine minutes late, and only 21½ miles to go, but driver and fireman went for it with a vengeance, and the result was one of the most exciting 20 minutes I have ever experienced on the footplate. The road from Girvan to Ayr is a heavily graded switchback, with downhill stretches preceding most of the steep climbs. With a 'Black Five' and only four coaches anything might seem possible, but because of curves and engineering restrictions there are not many places where one can run up to 70 mph. To a good driver bent on regaining lost time there was only one course open, to go hard uphill, and go hard we did! The start from Girvan in fearful weather set the standard. Up the Killochan bank, on 1 in 72, we accelerated to 55 mph on a bank as steep as Beattock; then 70 mph through Bargany, 60 over the crest at Dalquharran, and downhill, though steadily round the curves, to 'Ben's Cut', to pass Kilkerran, eight miles from Girvan, in 8¾ minutes. Up the heavy grade to Maybole we went, rounding the wide curve at 48 mph and then away again for a fast finish. Seventy-two miles an hour over the Doon viaduct below Cassillis, 60 over the peak at Dalrymple Junction, and with the lights of Ayr already in sight we passed Alloway Junction, 19½ miles in 19¾ minutes. A cautious run down the hill and we were at rest in Ayr in 22½ minutes from Girvan, only 1½ minutes late. It was journey's end for me that night, but I paused for a moment on that wet platform to wave Stroyan and McGhee away as they left for Glasgow, on time: a great run.

Not quite two years after that memorable run, on 28 October 1950 to be exact, there came the centenary of the Act of Incorporation of the old company, and it was marked by publication by the Stephenson Locomotive Society of a notable 60-page paperback, dedicated 'To the Immortal Memory of the Glasgow and South Western Railway and of all who served it'. It was a massively factual work of immense value to the historian, yet in its very seriousness conveying little or nothing of the spirit that animated every man-jack who worked on the line. It was Davie Smith in those inimitable *Railway Magazine* articles, subsequently republished in a handsomely illustrated book, who touched the heights in personal reminiscence. But it was when he and his father entertained me at their own fireside in Ayr that he amplified some of those amazing stories, filling in details that were a bit too hot for the sub-editors of *The Railway Magazine* and had received the Order of the Blue Pencil. The long wait out in the wilds at Glenwhilly on my own footplate run with the 'Glesca' Paddy' reminded me of one of his best stories – a railway comedy of errors if ever there was one. It should be explained that most of the drivers and firemen rarely went beyond Girvan, and when they got into the wild, bleak country to the south, on a pitch-black night with many toilsome miles between any lights that could give a clue to their whereabouts, some of them were 'very far from home', to quote Davie Smith's own words. And he himself must tell the tale of Glenwhilly, on a dark night back in 1926, when this particular pair were working their way home from Stranraer with a load of empty wagons.

'They were a long, long time climbing New Luce bank. Finally they got up, passed through Glenwhilly station, exchanged tablets and got the correct one for the next section, duly engraved "Glenwhilly–Barrhill". But the fireman looked at it, and he looked again, and he thought a bit and out on the dark moor doubts began to arise. He called to the driver, debate ensued, confusion became worse confounded. Finally they stopped and the fireman made his stumbling way back in the dark to the station. Glenwhilly is no Crewe or York. It boasts a staff of two only, and the station master was on duty in the box.

'Enter the fireman full of purpose. "You've given us the wrong tablet," said he.

'The station master seized the maligned token and examined it. " 'Glenwhilly–Barrhill' " he read. "What's wrong with that?"

' "It should be 'Barrhill–Pinwherry' " explained the fireman.

'For a few moments the station master stared,

In the very last days: in 1964 a southbound train of permanent way materials entering the Drumlanrig Gorge, Nith Valley line, hauled by a BR standard '5' 4–6–0 No. 73059   *Derek Cross*

then light began to dawn. "Where on earth do you think you are?" he demanded.

' "Barrhill," said the fireman. He was just 8½ miles out in his reckoning!'

But it was Davie and his father who told me the cream of the joke, unfortunately expunged by the editorial department of *The Railway Magazine*. A colleague of the bemused crew recalling the event said, 'They argued and they argued and then they gaed back to the station and the station master bloody near ett them!' Davie added a neat little press caption to the story: 'Attempted Cannibalism in the Wilds of Wigtownshire'.

The Wilds of Wigtownshire . . .! During the Second World War, when we were ensconced in our wartime base down in Wessex, and exhorted not to travel unless it was absolutely essential, we received an order for some mechanical signalling equipment that caused much perplexity to some of my colleagues. It was for Cairn Ryan. Where on earth was it? The job was cloaked in an unusual amount of secrecy, and I wondered what was happening at the settlement by the lighthouse, half-way to the open sea from Stranraer up the sheltered eight-mile-long inlet of Loch Ryan. The year was 1941, and in 'hush-hush' conditions ports were being built on the West Coast of Scotland to receive war material under the 'lease-lend' arrangement coming in from the USA. We learned afterwards that deep-water piers were being built by the Cairn Ryan lighthouse, with a full equipment of heavy lift cranes, and a branch-line railway was to be laid in from Stranraer to link up with a comprehensive nest of sidings on the level

Early one April morning in 1961: sleeping car express Euston to Glasgow (via Kilmarnock) at Polquhap summit hauled 4–6–2 engine No. 46232 *Duchess of Montrose*   *Derek Cross*

promontory just in-shore from the lighthouse. All the constructional work was being done by military labour, Royal Engineers and the Pioneer Corps, and the equipment ordered was of the simplest.

Apart from reflecting that Cairn Ryan was not exactly the easiest place from which to organize heavy freight movements by rail, with the one-time Joint Line through Galloway to Dumfries second only in severity to that of the 'Sou' West' line up to Ayr, the job passed from my mind; and it was not until some time after the war that I heard of an amusing side-kick. The military authorities obtained their permanent way equipment from the L M S, and in making the requisition it had been stated that there was no need for the sleepers to be creosoted. The line to the port would not be in use for more than a few years, and any deterioration of the timbers in that time would be slight and unimportant. But the railway people in meeting the requisition drew standard sleepers from store, realizing it would be far more trouble and more expensive to prepare untreated timbers. When the material arrived on the site, however, all hell was let loose, not so much because the specification had been disregarded, as that handling creosoted sleepers would soil the men's uniforms!

War years on the 'Sou' West' recall the running of the 'Ghost Train'. Despite governmental exhortations not to travel, passenger traffic between London and Scotland inevitably became very heavy. An enormous industrial effort became concentrated on Glasgow and the Clyde; there was much 'official' coming and going, not to mention service travel, leave and otherwise, to and from the numerous naval and military establishments on the West Coast, and the night trains especially became prodigiously heavy and at times insufferably crowded. Then one night a roving newspaper reporter at Euston discovered a heavy train, plentifully furnished with first-class sleeping cars, which was not in the public timetable. Intrigued, he went to Euston again, and discovered that it ran every night. The L M S was not playing the game, and though every other train leaving for the north was packed to repletion something had to be done

One of the ex-G & S W R Drummond express goods 2–6–0s, post-grouping, after transfer from Currock to the former Caledonian shed at Kingmoor   *O. S. Nock*

22

about it, and eventually a question was tabled in the House of Commons. It then transpired that the train was a 'special' reserved for Services personnel and others travelling on government business, and was available only to those carrying special permits.

It ran nightly between Euston and Glasgow St Enoch, and from its passengers' point of view was non-stop between Watford Junction and Dumfries, and similarly in the reverse direction. The only other intermediate stop between London and Glasgow was at Kilmarnock, which was convenient for the many wartime activities centred upon the Ayrshire coast. At the southern end,

Watford was the base of the L M S headquarters staff evacuated from their normal abode at Euston House. The 'Ghost Train', as it became known, ran until some time after the end of the war and in view of the interest in its working the L M S gave me a footplate pass to ride down from Glasgow to Carlisle one winter's night. Although the train was nominally non-stop from Dumfries to Watford and one 'Pacific' engine worked through from Glasgow to London, a stop was made abreast of Upperby Bridge running sheds, about a mile south of Carlisle Citadel station, for a change of enginemen. I boarded the *Princess Alexandra*, one of the streamlined 'Coronation' class, at St Enoch that night, and had a lovely run down to Carlisle;

Ex-G & S W R 0–6–2 tank engine No. 16902 after transfer to the Highland section at Blair Atholl for banking duties   *O.S.Nock*

but on joining the crew I was momentarily surprised to hear the broad, robust speech of West Cumberland. They were both ex-G & S W R men and like all their kind very proud of it, still bearing something of a grievance that so much of the old company's individualism had been subjugated to that of the Caledonian after the Grouping of 1923.

The abolition of their own engine shed in Carlisle was a case in point. The Glasgow and South Western was the second Scottish railway to arrive

24

in Carlisle. The Caledonian came first across the Border, and when the Sou' West obtained their authority it was to build a line only to Gretna and then to proceed, by your leave as it were, by running powers over the Caledonian line over the last eight miles. The two companies being so antagonistic, from management down to the humblest artisan, it was no more than natural that the Sou' West should establish their locomotive depot as far as possible from that of their rivals, to obviate any risk of sabotage! They hid it so successfully that very few travellers, even dedicated locomotive enthusiasts, knew where it was. Perhaps the most widely acclaimed railway photographer in pre-Grouping days was F. E. Mackay, who despite his name was a cheery little London cockney. I came to know him well, and I remember his telling me how once he walked the railway tracks around Carlisle searching for the Glasgow and South Western engine sheds. It had never occurred to him to extend his search down the Maryport and Carlisle line, for that is where they were, tucked away, and again reached only by running powers, at Currock. He never found them, and if you refer to the accompanying map you will

know why! The sheds were closed in 1924, and the engines and their men transferred to the Caledonian sheds. But the memory of them survives today. For on the site of Currock shed the Carlisle Corporation Electricity Undertaking built a substation, which they named G & S W R Substation – still used today – and the road that leads to it is called 'South Western Terrace'.

The most deadly blow in the remorseless process of expunging all memories of the G & S W from the life of the City of Glasgow was the closing and ultimate demolition of St Enoch station and the disposal of the hotel. Apart from the time when I worked in its precincts and was a frequent caller in the Divisional Engineer's offices alongside, I have two memories of the hotel. The first was near the end of the war when on my few free weekends I was doing some fieldwork for an assignment from *The Engineer*, and had spent about five hours on the footplate of an express from Leeds. It was late at night; I had a room reserved in the hotel, and I went straight from the engine to register. After I had signed in and got my room-key the pretty, soft-voiced Scots lassie behind the desk said, 'Ye'll no be wantin' a wash?' When I saw myself in a mirror I realized how indescribably dirty I had become in that five-hour footplate ride.

The second occasion was much later, in the lounge of the hotel. I had been dining with a retired civil engineer, Comyn McGregor, and enjoying his fund of railway stories. He was one of those remarkable men to whom railways were not only his chosen profession but an absolute way of life that continued after his retirement. Before Grouping he had been on the Caledonian, but the amalgamations of 1923 which brought the 'Sou' West' and the Highland also into the L M S gave him more scope to indulge one of his abiding ambitions, to *walk* over every mile of the railway. He had completed his perambulation of the entire Caledonian system long before, and he had later done the same with the Glasgow and South Western; but he had to admit that he had not yet finished the Highland.

There was a pause in our conversation, in which

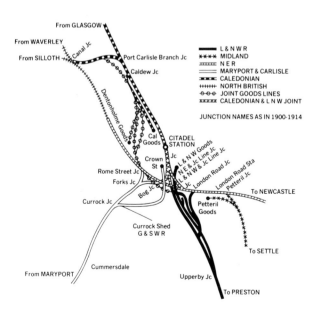

I happened involuntarily to be looking up at the lampshades below the ceiling of the room. He caught the direction of my gaze, and told me this story. Those shades took the form of an opaque spherical glass bowl, with a wide flat disc circling it on the centre line. One night, McGregor told me, he was sitting near a man who had imbibed considerably more than a 'wee dram' and who, quite bemused, was gazing steadfastly at one of those lampshades. After at least ten minutes, so McGregor assured me, he suddenly exclaimed: 'Got it; Saturn'!

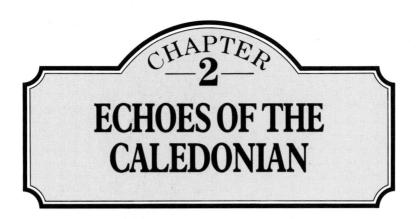

CHAPTER 2

ECHOES OF THE CALEDONIAN

For upwards of a quarter-century John Barr was a mighty power in the land at St Rollox. In McIntosh's day he was already a senior Running Officer, and when Lord Monkswell was accorded the privilege of a footplate pass from Glasgow to Aberdeen and back in 1913, and the occasion was important enough for McIntosh himself to leave his headquarters office and come down to Buchanan Street station to see them off, Barr rode on the footplate with the noble visitor. Lord Monkswell had written with the utmost enthusiasm of the great days of the early 'Dunala-stairs', going so far as to hold them up as the only British locomotives at the turn of the century that could match the work of the de Glehn compound express engines on the Northern Railway of France. But in 1913, while the presence of Barr on the footplate was a guarantee that the engines would be efficiently handled, Lord Monkswell does not seem to have been very impressed. The engines on which he rode were a 5ft 9in. 4–6–0 No. 913 from Glasgow to Perth, a superheated 'Dunala-stair IV' class 4–4–0 No. 132 from Perth to Aberdeen and back, and finally the magnificent express 4–6–0 No. 50 *Sir James Thompson* from Perth to Glasgow. One searches his travelling diary in vain for any significant details of the work, because from the baldest notes it would seem that much of the running was very fine, and

between Glasgow and Perth particularly much better than that with which we were served up in L M S days.

Technicalities apart, however, what a feast of nostalgia even the contemplation of such a round of footplate riding arouses. Those great blue engines, with their gorgeous colouring and spotless turnout, were one of the great sights of the British railways in pre-Grouping days; yet Lord Monkswell passed a day in their most intimate company without a word on the beauty of their appearance. Footplate passes were not lightly granted on the Caledonian. When the late E. C. Poultney, the well-known engineer–author, asked for one about the same time, McIntosh laughed his request away, saying, 'Och, ye'd fall off!' Barr came into the picture once again in Lord Monkswell's diaries when a footplate pass was granted to ride the first of the Pickersgill three-cylinder 4–6–0s, in September 1922. Apparently they made an even more special occasion of it than with the noble lord's trip to Aberdeen in 1913. The engine itself, No. 956, was shedded at Balornock, and normally worked between Glasgow (Buchanan Street) and Perth, and she was brought over to south of the city to work the up 'Corridor' – the afternoon express for London – down to Carlisle, and to return with the corresponding north-bound train leaving Carlisle at 7.50 p.m. This

again was a special assignment because the normal working was for the engine of the 3.50 p.m. up for Glasgow to work back from Carlisle on the down 'Corridor'.

The Pickersgill three-cylinder 4–6–0s 956–9 were probably the greatest enigmas in locomotive design that have ever run the rails in Great Britain. How a locomotive establishment with the towering status of St Rollox could have produced four such bad engines is beyond belief. For Lord Monkswell's trip from Glasgow to Carlisle and back the regular driver of No. 956 was brought over from Balornock, James Grassie, one of the ablest of Scottish enginemen. He had driven the beautiful McIntosh 4–6–0 No. 50 on Lord Monkswell's 1913 round trip to Aberdeen. At the height of the troubles with the big Pickersgill three-cylinder 4–6–0s it was said that Grassie was the only man who could do anything with them;

but even with Barr at his elbow and his distinguished visitor noting points he did not do very well on that September day in 1922, and Lord Monkswell summed it up in two sentences. 'The work was poor throughout. The trouble was primarily that the engine would not steam.' Actually, I believe there was a good deal more to it than that; but there is no point in prolonging what would be an unhappy echo of the Caledonian. In later years I met both Barr and James Grassie, and have the liveliest recollections of their vivid personalities.

In 1934 in connection with some of my earliest work as a technical journalist I had an engine pass

Caley 4–4–0s in the Highlands: a Pickersgill 4–4–0
No. 54482 assists a 'Black Five' 4–6–0 with a train
of locomotive coal for Inverness, on the steep ascent
to Slochd summit. No. 54482 as C R No. 77 was
built in 1920 and not scrapped until 42 years later

W. J. V. Anderson

to make the same round trip that Lord Monkswell enjoyed in 1913. Some considerable tightening up of the express train schedules over the Aberdeen route had taken place, and with the continued use of ex-Caledonian engines my friends at Euston House, L M S headquarters, were anxious for a little publicity in that direction. The 10 a.m. express from Glasgow (Buchanan Street) had recently been distinguished by being named 'The Granite City', and then made its first stop at Gleneagles, 47½ miles, in 69 minutes. It was booked to pass Stirling, 30¼ miles, in 43 minutes, 2½ minutes more than Lord Monkswell had noted in 1913; but interest lay in the use of the Pickersgill type of 4–4–0, easily the best design that engineer produced. Their value as medium-power motive power units was emphasized by their long life, because the engine I rode from Glasgow that morning, No. 14488, built in 1921 as Caledonian No. 83, was not withdrawn from service until 1961, 27 years after I rode on her. The second one, on to which I changed at Perth on that same day, lasted nearly as long, until 1960. The performances did not come up to the expectations of the enthusiastic publicity folks in London, and I could not make much of a story out of their running.

Fortunately the day's recording was only half over when I reached Aberdeen, and returning to Glasgow I had a rare treat. It is true that the engine for the southbound 'Granite City' express was a Midland compound and not a Caledonian, but the driver was none other than James Grassie, still driving fast expresses more than 20 years after Lord Monkswell had first made his acquaintance. The Midland compound No. 1127 was a lovely engine, and gave us a superb run. Although only a 4–4–0 she had a tractive force greater than the big 4–6–0 No. 50 that Grassie had driven in 1913, 22,649 lb against 21,348 lb, and she was a fine hillclimber. The speed she made on the faster stretches also was exhilarating and in contrast to the great three-cylinder 4–6–0 No. 956, which made such heavy weather of the Carlisle run for Lord Monkswell, the compound steamed with the utmost freedom. The original Caledonian 4–4–0s,

of both McIntosh and Pickersgill design, were largely superseded by the Midland compounds in the late 1920s on the more important express passenger trains, but they still had a notable part to play in Scottish train service operation.

When I was doing the research for my book about the Caledonian Railway (published by Ian Allan Ltd in 1961) I had the privilege of visiting John Barr in his home in Newlands, among the southern suburbs of Glasgow. Though he had retired many years previously he was still hale and hearty and had a fund of reminiscence. Like Comyn McGregor, to him the Caledonian Railway and all its affairs were the very breath of life. I gathered that after the forthright and dynamic J. F. McIntosh he found Pickersgill a bit difficult. It was not that he was an awkward or self-willed man – rather the reverse. The trouble was to get him to make a decision. He had a kindly and gentle nature, and although a scholarly man he shrank from making decisions that appeared to override the susceptibilities of any of his staff. In consequence the engines that were designed under his general direction were an extraordinary mixture of good and bad. When Grouping came in 1923, and the supreme command of mechanical engineering affairs on the L M S passed first of all to Horwich and then to Derby, John Barr fought a tremendous battle in upholding the merits of Caledonian engines, and it was through his staunch advocacy that 4–4–0s and 4–6–0s of the Pickersgill type were subjected to dynamometer car testing in competition with Midland and London and North Western locomotives. They did not come out of it very well so far as coal consumption and maximum performance were concerned; but many years after those tests I was interested to hear Barr uphold the Pickersgill 4–4–0s: 'They were our best engines.'

I went away from that pleasant interview to give his words much thought. At that time only one out of the forty-eight Pickersgill 4–4–0s had been scrapped and that one would have survived as long as the others but for involvement in the apocalyptic head-on collision at Gollanfield Junction, in 1953, in which she was reduced to little more than scrap iron. But by the late autumn of 1959, when the first of the working Pickersgills was called in for scrapping, fewer than a dozen out of the 240 Midland compounds remained, and their fiery brilliant partners in the pre-Grouping West Coast Anglo-Scottish service, the L N W R 'George the Fifth' class 4–4–0s, had long since disappeared. I studied drawings and statistics of performance; not performance in the sense of sustained power output in heavy passenger traffic, but in maintenance costs and freedom from casualty, and then the sterling worth of the Pickersgills, and little less those of the McIntosh engines that preceded them, began to come clear.

Under L M S management, in order to segregate the 'sheep' from the 'goats' in the total locomotive stock a system of individual costing was instituted in which the money spent on repairs for every individual engine was recorded, and that spent on coal and oil recorded separately. Then the aggregate figures for each engine class were totalled up, and presented to management on a comparative basis. The class with the lowest total of repair costs was given the index number 100, and a class which had an average cost per engine 50 per cent greater than the lowest was registered as having a repair cost index of 150, and so, proportionately, through all the principal classes in the total locomotive stock. The lowest class in these exhaustive analyses, which were based on statistics amassed over a lengthy period, was the Midland type No. 2 class 4–4–0. This was a light power unit, soundly designed, but proving light on repairs partly

Caley 4–4–0s in the Highlands: one of the last 'Dunalastair IV' class to survive: No. 54458, built as No. 41 in 1914, photographed at Dingwall in 1956   *J. L. Stevenson*

because the engines concerned had a relatively low load rating and were rarely called upon for really hard work. But the Pickersgill 4–4–0s came next in the scale, with a repair cost index of 110, against 136 for a Midland Compound, 149 for an L N W R 'George the Fifth' 4–4–0, or no less than 190 for one of the deadly rival Glasgow and South Western 4–6–0s. The Pickersgill 4–4–0, although heavy on coal when pushed to its limit with a heavy train, was clearly a sound economic proposition to maintain, for a medium power engine for secondary passenger services.

The low repair cost index of these engines was due to their massive frame construction and generous bearing surfaces. The McIntosh superheater 4–4–0s of the 'Dunalastair IV' series, which were excellent engines in traffic and lasted until the mid-1950s, had main frames $1\frac{1}{16}$ in. thick. The Pickersgill had $1\frac{1}{4}$ in. thick frames, and backed up by considerably larger bearing surfaces it might seem that they were intended to last for ever! Some comparative dimensions are interesting, as shown in Table 1. Critics might have argued that the Pickersgills were unduly heavy for the work they were designed to do; but those massive frames and large bearings paid off in their longevity of service.

Table 1

Class	Dunalastair IV		Pickers-gill
Crankpins			
diameter × length (in.)	$9\frac{1}{4} \times 4$		$9\frac{1}{2} \times 4\frac{1}{2}$
Driving axle bearings			
diameter × length (in.)	$9\frac{1}{4} \times 7\frac{1}{2}$		$9\frac{1}{2} \times 9$
Trailing axle bearings	curved	waisted	parallel
diameter × length (in.)	$9\frac{1}{4}$ max.	$7\frac{3}{4}$ min.	$8\frac{1}{4} \times 12$

In the later 1920s I came to know well a young engineer who, after a pupilship in the Midland Railway works at Derby and much footplate experience on ordinary service trains and in dynamometer car testing, had forsaken the practical side of the profession and joined the staff of the Institution of Mechanical Engineers in an editorial capacity. We used to foregather after meetings and yarn about locomotives, and I went occasionally to his home in South London. He was brilliant technically and, in his earlier days, when footplating, usually persuaded the driver to let him take the regulator instead of the more usual role of a pupil which was relieving the fireman of the job of shovelling coal! But he had been one of the dynamometer car crew in the comparative tests made between Carlisle and Leeds at the end of 1924, when in response to the stout advocacy of John Barr a Pickersgill 4–4–0 was included. It was not altogether a fair trial. In the new L M S power classification the Caledonian engine was in the No. 3 class and, according to Midland loading limits for the trains in question, would not have been permitted to take more than 230 tons without a pilot engine to assist; but the test load was 300 tons, and it presented a tremendous challenge to engine and crew.

My ex-Derby friend, like most of his kind in that era, was apt to look with complete disdain upon most engines that were not of Midland origin, and he was scathing beyond words about that overloaded, overextended Pickersgill 4–4–0, which he stigmatized as 'the world's worst'. The return trip to Carlisle had been made on the 4.03 p.m. express from Leeds, in December after dark for the whole distance, and he described to me in vivid terms the awe-inspiring sight of the Caledonian engine pounding its way from Settle Junction up to Blea Moor, at little below 30 mph on the long 1 in 100 gradient. He recalled how, in the darkness, the exhaust from the chimney looked like a solid mass of *flame*, so thick were the red-hot cinders being flung out, and how the fireman was shovelling for dear life. Actually, on a relatively small grate the physical work would not have been unduly

---

A Pickersgill 4–4–0 No. 54494, built as No. 89 in 1921, on a southbound goods train near Murthly, Perthshire. This engine was not withdrawn until 1960   *W. J. V. Anderson*

arduous. The engine steamed extremely well, but the limit had been reached at which the cylinders could make use of the steam generated. But a Midland No. 3 class engine would not have been able to get anywhere near what the Pickersgill did. As to the look of the exhaust I am reminded of the laconic comment of another Scottish driver following a hard run he had made on the previous evening: 'Some o' the sparks are no' doon yet!'

'The Caledonian' – high speed train of the last days of steam, heading south near Tebay, Cumbria, in wintry weather, hauled by 'Duchess' class 4–6–2 No. 46236 *City of Bradford*   *Derek Cross*

At the time of the Grouping, in 1923, John Barr was appointed Motive Power Superintendent for Scotland, on the L M S, and he soon had to provide for the running of faster and heavier trains. The allocation of many new Midland compounds to Scottish sheds certainly helped, and in 1927 there came the 'Royal Scots'; but in the meantime Barr had secured the building, in 1925, of twenty more 4–6–0s of Pickersgill's outside cylinder design, which had been introduced in 1916. The new engines were all built at St Rollox Works, and painted magnificently in Midland red. Earlier that year a little-known but very important and objective series of competitive trials had been carried out between Carlisle and Preston, with London and North Western, Midland, and Lancashire and Yorkshire engines. It was only quite by accident that I learned in the following year that one of the new Pickersgill 4–6–0s had been put through in the same testing routine. When we were living at Bushey in the early 1930s I used occasionally to visit some friends, a widow and her daughter, who to eke out their modest income had a paying guest, a railwayman on the L M S. Knowing of my own interest in railways they tried to arrange a meeting, but somehow it never came off. The only contact was to be shown, on one of my visits, a large photograph album containing, believe it or not, a series of snapshots showing the first of the new Caledonian 4–6–0s, No. 14630, with the Horwich dynamometer car during the tests made in June 1926 between Carlisle and Preston. I gathered, however, that the album had been extracted from its owner's effects surreptitiously and no mention was subsequently made of it – more's the pity.

It was not until some 30 years later that the Chief Mechanical Engineer of the London Midland Region permitted me to study the results of those Carlisle–Preston trials of 1925–6, and I found then that the Caledonian 4–6–0 engine had done well in climbing the banks, but at the expense of heavy coal consumption. Like Pickersgill's 4–4–0s they were strongly built engines with a low repair cost index, but they had no turn of speed, and consequently made a relatively poor showing in express passenger traffic. I travelled a number of times behind them between Glasgow and Perth, and while they climbed the Gleneagles bank, from the Perth side, in good style they rarely much exceeded 50 mph on the level stretches. As more and more new engines became available Barr deployed the ex-Caledonian units to locations far beyond their original haunts, and some of the Pickersgill 4–6–0s were transferred to the Glasgow and South Western line. Antagonism towards anything connected with the Caledonian continued long after the two great rivals had been absorbed into the L M S, and the traditional sluggishness of the Pickersgill 4–6–0s led to the 'Sou' West' men nicknaming them the 'Greybacks' – in other words, the louses! Be that as it may, I have heard of a 'Sou' West' man getting 77 mph out of one of them, on a level track too.

The antagonism to all things Caledonian was dying out on the Glasgow and South Western line in the 1930s. Their own engines, not so robustly built, were being replaced and, 'Greybacks' apart, the Caledonians were being appreciated. At Easter 1932 while staying at Dumfries I travelled to Newton Stewart to make a tramp towards the Galloway Highlands. My train was hauled, in dashing style, by a little Caley 'Jumbo' 0–6–0, and at Newton Stewart we were to 'cross' the 9.20 a.m. up from Stranraer. On it came, not a G & S W R engine, but a non-superheated 'Dunalastair IV' 4–4–0 that had recently become domiciled in 'Sou' West' territory. It was symptomatic of a general replacement of the 'natives' by the smaller and older Caledonian 4–4–0s, although at Newton Stewart the appearance of engine No. 14359 (formerly C R No. 150) was not really as incongruous as it might seem. This line, in pre-Grouping days, was a joint affair, not only of the G & S W and the Caledonian but also of the London and North Western and the Midland. It was completely encompassed by purely G & S W R lines at Castle Douglas, its eastern extremity, and at Challoch Junction where the line from Girvan joined. Until the 1930s nearly all the trains had been worked by G & S W engines.

By then 'echoes of the Caledonian' in the form of the strident exhaust beats of its locomotives began

to be heard more and more in south-west Scotland, and at one time engines of the second 'Dunalastair' series, dating back to 1897, were used on the prestigious evening boat train from Glasgow to Stranraer, for the night service to Belfast. This train ran the 37.9 miles from Girvan to Stranraer Harbour in 67 minutes non-stop. This might not seem much of an express run, but when the difficulties of the route are borne in mind (as exemplified by my own footplate experience related in the preceding chapter), one appreciates that it required skilful enginemanship and first-class locomotive performance. Although the loads were not heavy, generally less than 200 tons, the train provided no mean task for engines of 1897 vintage when gradients of 1 in 54 and 1 in 57 had to be mounted. Two runs with this train gave overall times of $64\frac{1}{4}$ and $64\frac{3}{4}$ minutes from Girvan to Stranraer, and when those little engines were pounding up the 1 in 70 gradients on either side of Barrhill at little below 30 mph one may be sure there were 'echoes of the Caledonian' to be heard. The 'Dunalastair IV' that I saw at Newton Stewart in 1932 also gave Davie Smith a splendid run on the 7.30 p.m. from Stranraer Town to Girvan about the same time.

The Second World War brought little diminution in the ranks of these sturdy 4–4–0 engines; but in 1948 when nationalization of the railways came and there was much talk of modernization it did seem that their days were surely numbered. At that time, however, all but one of the superheated 'Dunalastair IV' class and all the forty-eight Pickersgills were still in service, and while at the end of the war they were mostly in old Caledonian territory the migration north was soon to begin. When my publisher friend Ronald Nelson asked me to do a book about 'Scottish Railways' and determined that it should contain no fewer than fourteen colour plates showing locomotives in various stages in their history – right down to the colours adopted in the earliest days of British Railways – we felt that as the solitary survivor in Caledonian blue the old single-wheeler of 1888, No. 123, must be included. She was then deeply ensconced in St Rollox Works, out of harm's way it had been hoped during the war, and she was by no means in pristine condition. After her preservation had been secured, in 1933, and she had been repainted no one seemed to know quite what to do with her. There was no room in the only railway museum then in existence, at York, and she virtually disappeared from public gaze. In 1948, however, we obtained permission to have her extracted to be photographed in colour for the Nelson book, and she was nicely cleaned up for the occasion. But then she went inside again.

Later in that year, however, Caledonian locomotives came into the picture once again in rather unexpected circumstances. After the scrapping of a number of the old Highland engines some of the Pickersgill 4–4–0s based at Perth were sent to Blair Atholl to provide rear-end banking assistance when required on 'The Hill' – the tremendous climb, mostly on gradients of 1 in 70, from Struan up to Dalnaspidal. The booked times of passenger trains then in operation required sustained speeds of 25–30 mph up that long bank, and assistance was given to the Stanier 'Black Five' 4–6–0s when the load exceeded 255 tons. Then came the locomotive interchange trials instituted by the newly formed Railway Executive of the nationalized British Railways, and 'B1' 4–6–0s of L N E R design and the Bulleid 'air-smoothed' 'Pacifics' of the 'West Country' class were put into competition with the 'Black Fives'. On certain routes also the ex-Great Western 'Halls' were also involved, but because of loading gauge restrictions these latter engines were not permitted to run in Scotland. The Highland line between Perth and Inverness was one of the chosen routes for testing, and as the test load was fixed at 350 tons the Pickersgill 4–4–0s were called upon to assist up 'The Hill'. The dynamometer car was placed between the engine under test and the

'The Caledonian' at high speed near Kings Langley, Herts, hauled by engine No. 46244 *King George VI*
British Railways

train, so that it recorded only the work that the test engine was doing; but a careful comparison of the horsepowers recorded in the car and the total effort required to haul the train up the gradient enables a close estimate to be made of what the bank engine in rear was doing.

Where hard slogging on heavy gradients is concerned, with these engines one's thoughts always go back to those murderous test runs on the Midland in December 1924, and engine No. 124, then still resplendent in Caledonian blue, produced a maximum equivalent drawbar horsepower of 870 at a speed of 27 mph. Five records taken in 1948 on 'The Hill' gave figures of 655, 595, 645, 620 and 720 equivalent drawbar horsepower, so that these thirty-year-old Pickersgills were doing no mean job of work in assisting the test engines, and it was soon evident that they had come to stay in the Highlands. In 1954 there were nine of them at Perth, covering the southern end of the line, three at Aviemore, four at Forres, four at Inverness, two at Helmsdale and one at the furthest tip of the line, at Wick. At the same time Aviemore also had one of the superheated 'Dunalastair IV's; Inverness had two more of them, and there was yet another up at Wick. One of the Inverness DIVs No. 54455 was indeed a battle-scarred veteran, for as Caledonian Railway No. 48, in 1915, she was the second engine of the Euston to Glasgow sleeper that ran at full speed into the wreck of the troop train at Quintinshill, and added to the carnage among the men of the Royal Scots who had survived the first collision. None of the five 'Dunalastair IV's on the Highland survived long after 1954, but withdrawal of the Pickersgills, except for the one destroyed in the Gollanfield head-on collision in 1953, did not commence until 1959.

The twenty-two Pickersgills that survived on

The down mail leaving Dalwhinnie hauled by two ex-Caledonian Pickersgill 4–4–0s Nos. 54485 and 54486, formerly Caledonian Nos. 80 and 81, built in 1920
W. J. V. Anderson

the Highland line, of which the majority lasted into the 1960s, became much appreciated engines in that difficult country. They worked some of the short-distance local trains, but they were found very useful in assisting on the main-line expresses. The Stanier 'Black Five' 4–6–0s were of course the standard engines for all through traffic, and before the introduction of the Pickersgills it was customary to use a pair of 'Black Fives' on trains that needed double-heading. But there were few trains that needed the full tractive power of two such engines, and the combination of a Class '3' 4–4–0 and a 4–6–0 was ideal. In their last years the Pickersgills strongly upheld the old Caledonian reputation for smart appearance. It is true they were painted black, but returning periodically to their mother works, St Rollox, they were returned to the Highland in the lined-black livery that was an echo of their one-time English partner, the London and North Western. Thus arrayed, and kept looking spick and span, they double-headed all sorts of trains, from Anglo-Scottish expresses to the car-sleeper trains, and loads of locomotive coal being hauled up to Inverness.

In the summer of 1957 British Railways put on a new express service between Euston and Glasgow covering the 401 miles in 410 minutes, inclusive of one intermediate stop at Carlisle. It was the fastest train ever run over this route since the short-lived 'Coronation Scot' of 1937, and the booked average speed between Carlisle and Euston was 61.6 mph. By that time in British Railways' history the phase of officially denigrating all that had happened in the past was fading, and in a happy gesture the new train was named 'The Caledonian'. It carried a fine headboard on the smokebox of the locomotive, surmounted by the crosses of St Andrew and St George, in colour. It was a time when preparations for electrification

The famous Caledonian 4–2–2 engine No. 123, in her last days as an ordinary traffic department engine, painted plain black, numbered 14010, and stationed at Perth in 1932   *O. S. Nock*

of the line south of Crewe were beginning, and much work had to be done on the track, with consequent imposition of many temporary speed restrictions. Although the 'Duchess' class 'Pacific' engines were used on this fast train it was thought desirable to limit the load to eight coaches so as to give a good margin of power in reserve for making up lost time. In the summer of 1958 I had a good run on the southbound 'Caledonian', which nevertheless showed up many of the difficulties that British Railways were experiencing in trying to keep a good passenger train service going while modernization plans were involving much civil engineering work on the line.

'The Caledonian' put on a brave show that day. Hauled by a resplendent engine, the *City of Chester*, we were only four minutes late away from Carlisle, and despite numerous hindrances to fast running on the non-stop journey of nearly 300 miles we had recovered all the lost time when Harrow was passed, 288 miles from Carlisle in 255¼ minutes; but the work in rebuilding Euston had meant that a number of the platforms were out of action, and we had to wait outside for more than 10 minutes before one of them was clear for us to run in. But that was no fault of our fine engine and its crew, which had brought us along fully in the style of that once famous Caledonian poster. Before the railway became part of the L M S its publicity department adorned the walls of many of its stations with a very attractive series of posters, some of which advertised the scenic beauties of the line, others the various golf courses that it serviced, but there was one that specially took my eye. There was no picture, just this wording:

> *Punctuality is the courtesy of Kings.*
> *It marks the line that leads to England.*

I thought of that poster as the 'Caledonian' was racing its way through the midland shires of Eng-

---

The first of the Pickersgill two-cylinder 4–6–0s of Caledonian design, built for the L M S after grouping: No. 14631, at Kingmoor shed, Carlisle   *O. S. Nock*

land in the hope of making a punctual arrival in London.

The year 1958 was a Caledonian landmark in another respect, for it was then that the preserved 4–2–2 single driving-wheel locomotive No. 123 was restored to full working order; not only so, but she proved to be in such excellent working condition that for the first time in her long life she steamed south of the Border, on many special train assignments, and enthusiasts far and wide were able to enjoy the beauty of an engine immaculately turned out in 'Caley Blue', as we knew it of old. Of course a small engine, with no more than a single pair of driving wheels and thus with limited adhesion, could not haul very heavy trains, and usually she worked in partnership with larger engines. These, thanks to the inspiration of the reigning General Manager of the Scottish Region of British Railways, James Ness, were usually other vintage Scottish locomotives that had been preserved, put into full working order and painted in their old pre-Grouping colours. Wherever she went, sometimes even in partnership with the Great Western hundred-mile-an-hour-er *City of Truro*, the dazzling blue Caledonian '123' led the way.

Towards the end of 1961 I went to Inverness to begin research for my book *The Highland Railway* (published by Ian Allan Ltd, 1965). By then the diesels had taken over the main-line workings and on a morning when the high mountains were deep in snow I rode the engine of the mail northwards from Perth. On arrival at Inverness my work was mainly in the archives, rummaging through some incredibly dusty old files, but there was time to walk out to what was once the most picturesque of running sheds, the roundhouse in the precincts of which so many Highland engines had posed for their photographs. The folding doors behind which the older engines used to be tucked away from the cold had long disappeared. They went out of use when the 4–6–0s with their big eight-wheeled tenders were longer than the tracks inside the shed, but the fine stone archways leading in had remained. But when I was there in November 1961 the first stages of total demolition had begun, and naught but slender steel stanchions supported the roof. The 'Black Five' 4–6–0s that were once the standard main-line power on the Highland had all gone, but not the Pickersgills. Three of them had been withdrawn from traffic and were in store, but another three were on the shed and *in steam*.

One of these latter was none other than 54466, which as Caledonian No. 124 was tested between Carlisle and Leeds in 1924 and put up such a noble fight against heavy odds, while one of those in store, No. 54463 (C R No. 115) had hauled the prestigious 1.30 p.m. West Coast 'Corridor' express from Glasgow down to Carlisle when I was a passenger in 1923. Two of those 'in store' when I was in Inverness in 1961 did no further work, but looking upon the others on that sunny November day I was moved to whisper to myself the old Scots saying: 'Lang may your lums reek!' (Long may your chimneys smoke.) Actually, however, all three of those working Pickersgills were taken out of service in the following March; but 54463 (C R 115) lasted until December 1962, to become the final survivor, at the good old age (for a locomotive) of forty-six years.

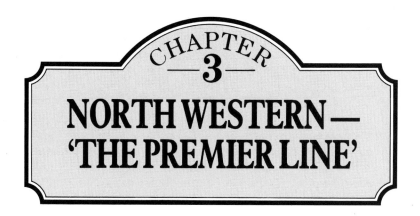

CHAPTER
—3—
NORTH WESTERN—
'THE PREMIER LINE'

The London and North Western and Caledonian Railways were close and cordial partners in the operation of the West Coast route; but at the turn of the century it was whispered that Caledonian drivers with the highly prized 'Dunalastair' 4–4–0s had acquired such a superiority complex over all other users of the Citadel station in Carlisle that they did not deign to acknowledge their North Western partners when they coupled off on arrival from the south. So much, in their eyes, for the railway that regarded itself as 'The Premier Line'! In business and financial circles the position of the North Western was universally acknowledged, and then it was indeed the largest joint stock corporation in the world, with its ordinary shares regarded as near to gilt-edged securities. When I became closely aware of it in the early 1920s things were somewhat in suspense, and the early Grouping years were to bring cataclysmic changes in both management principles and day-to-day working. How the warring factions were gradually co-ordinated and welded into the strong team that carried the L M S through the war years is a heart-warming story but outside the scope of this book.

The West Coast main line took a terrible beating in the war years. The traffic it carried was prodigious, and although a limitation was placed on the maximum speed of passenger trains the state of the track became such that many more temporary restrictions had to be imposed than were normal. Even though train schedules were much slower than those of pre-war days, there were so many lengths of line over which speed had to be kept low that timekeeping was often very bad. Then to crown all came the fearful winter of 1946–7, which, added to the arrears of maintenance that had accrued from the war years, had a positively devastating effect on all the most heavily used sections of the line south of Preston. The situation had barely begun to recover when nationalization of the railways took effect in January 1948; and when the locomotive interchange trials were conducted in April and May of that year, so far as the Euston–Carlisle route was concerned the once 'Premier Line' was still so infested with speed restrictions that the running of the test trains was some of the most disappointing in the whole series of trials. Furthermore, even several years after the end of the war the line was still congested with troop specials and other government traffic, which often had to be given priority over the ordinary express passenger trains.

In the early 1950s, however, there came a most remarkable recovery, and it was then that those of us who were able to travel frequently were to witness and record for posterity the thrilling, magnificent and deeply significant last days of steam on the West Coast main line. For they were indeed the last days. In 1955 the great government plan for the modernization of British Railways had been launched and this, of course, included as one of its most important features the total abolition of steam traction throughout the country. The West Coast main line, at any rate that portion of it from Euston to Weaver Junction (en route for Liverpool), was to be electrified, and although the 'last days' extended eventually to 1968, the civil engineering preparations for the much faster running that was contemplated produced a virtual stranglehold on the passenger service. In any case, before the end of the 1950s diesel–electric locomotives had begun to replace steam on some of the most important duties. So far as the longer distance express services were concerned the part played in my boyhood days by the L N W R 'George the Fifth' and 'Claughton' classes was, in the 1950s, being taken by the 'Converted Scots', and 'Princess Royal' and 'Duchess' class 'Pacifics'. The 'Princess Royal' class, only twelve strong and dating from 1933, had acquired the affectionate nickname of the 'Lizzies', from the monumental exploits of the second engine of the class, No. 6201 *Princess Elizabeth* in 1936.

The 'Converted Scots', the first of which had been so treated in 1943, were virtually new engines. The process of 'conversion' went on at intervals until 1955, by which time all the seventy engines of the class had been treated. The only parts of the original engines to remain were the frames, the wheel centres and the cabs. From the viewpoint of tractive power and thermodynamic performance they were new engines, but from the maintenance angle I have always understood that they showed some definite economies. In traffic, within my own experience, they gave very mixed results. J. F. Harrison, who was transferred from the Eastern Region to become Chief Mechanical Engineer of the London Midland, always said that they were 'our best engines'; but unfortunately I could not agree with him! Moreover, I do not think that many of the running inspectors would have agreed with his assessment either. He was prob-

ably thinking of his repair costs and not with knowledge of day-to-day performance on the road; because while the 'Converted Scots' at their best were very fine engines indeed, the times when they were not at their best were, in my experience, all too frequent. To reduce the amount of maintenance work needed when they were on shed the so-called self-cleaning screen filters had been fitted in the smoke boxes, and these, it was thought, had upset the balance between the draught-inducing effect of the blast pipe and the free-gas area through the boiler tubes. Some of my own experiences when travelling were such as to suggest that the boilers were not steaming freely.

Seeing that the new diesels would probably be taking over their work in a very few years it would seem that the simplest way out would have been to eschew the relatively slight economies in maintenance costs and take the self-cleaning screens out; but with complaints persisting, one of these engines was taken out of traffic and sent for thorough examination at the Rugby experimental testing station. There, the objective and strictly disciplined analysis carried out in 1955 showed that interposing the screens reduced the steaming capacity of the boiler, at maximum evaporation, by no more than 6 per cent, and because the ordinary demands made upon the engines in traffic were far below this theoretical maximum the presence of the plates should not make much difference. A major point made in the report eventually submitted by Rugby was that the fire-grate was very small in relation to the work the engines were expected to do. It is true that these engines had a nominal tractive effort roughly equal to that of the Gresley non-streamlined 'Pacifics', which had a grate area of 41 sq. ft against $31\frac{1}{4}$ sq. ft on the 'Scots'. On the other hand the Great Western 'Kings', which had a tractive effort far exceeding that of either, had a grate area of only 34 sq. ft. Moreover the 'Scots', even when pressed to maximum evaporation, were not excessive coal burners; and it was not as if any change could be made to this basic feature of the engine design. I

must admit I found this particular report rather unrealistic.

The 'Scots' at their best were capable of very fine work, and their quality did not deteriorate at the time when the diesels were gradually taking over. It was interesting also that there seemed little discernible difference between the maximum efforts of those that were replacements of the original 'Royal Scots' and had 18-in. diameter cylinders, and those that were reboilered 'Baby Scots' and had 17-in. diameter cylinders. In fact, one of the finest runs I have ever seen with an engine of either variety was made by one of the 17-in. series. From actual observation on the line it would certainly seem that the boiler and firebox, which were the subject of the critically adverse comment in the Rugby report, were the strength rather than the weakness of these engines. The run in question was made on the up 'Midday Scot' when engine No. 45530 had to take over haulage

On Shap in the last days of steam, the Liverpool–Glasgow express hauled by 4–6–0 No. 46107 *Argyll and Sutherland Highlander*, climbing the bank, passing the up 'Midday Scot', hauled by one of the '40' class diesels   *Derek Cross*

of a fourteen-coach train at Crewe, 483 tons tare, with a very crowded passenger complement about 530 tons full. I do not know what the official loading limit was for Class '7' engines, but when in 1932 the L M S took what the late Cecil J. Allen once called 'the venturesome step' of booking the 6.12 p.m. express over the 152.7 miles from Crewe to Willesden Junction non-stop in 142 minutes, a special range of loading limits called the 'XL' was introduced, and the maximum to be taken by a 'Royal Scot' was laid down as 380 tons. Yet on this run with engine No. 45530 in the last days of steam, not only was a load 103 tons heavier taken without assistance but the 'venturesome' schedule of 1932 had been bettered by 2½ minutes as early in the journey as Nuneaton. A signal check at Rugby cost 2 minutes, and even though the effort was relaxed a little after Bletchley, with the train getting ahead of time, the 158.1-mile run from Crewe to Euston was completed in 151 minutes, showing an actual average speed of 62.8 mph.

It is interesting to compare the booked times of 1932 with the actual times made in the late 1950s, as shown in Table 2. This run by engine No. 45530 was representative of the swansong of Class '7' locomotive running south of Crewe, because soon afterwards the preparations for electrification began in earnest. The siting and erection of overhead structures to carry the conductor wires were a relatively small item. The road bed over practically the entire distance had to be renewed, and built to withstand the far higher speeds that were contemplated. It was virtually a case of building an entirely new railway over the route of the old one, while, incidentally, the old one was carrying the most intense traffic of any main line in Great

Table 2

Distance (miles)		1932 schedule Max. tare load 380 tons (mins)	Actual times Tare load 483 tons (min./sec.)	
0.0	Crewe	0	0	00
24.5	Stafford	26	26	38
61.0	Nuneaton	60	57	28
–		–	sig. check	
75.5	Rugby	73	71	08
98.2	Roade	94	94	39*
114.4	Bletchley	105	105	03*
126.4	Tring	119	119	15*
152.7	Willesden Jn.	142 (stop)	142	26* (pass)
158.1	Euston	–	150	59*

* Net times allowing for Rugby check: 2 min. less.

One of the last L N W R engine class to remain in first class traffic: a 'Super D' 0–8–0 passing Lancaster, with a Class 'B' express goods train

Derek Cross

At New Cumnock watertroughs: a northbound banana special, hauled by 'Black Five' 4-6-0 No. 45138, in August 1965
Derek Cross

At Glenwhilly: two magnificently preserved locomotives, the Highland 'Jones Goods' No. 103, and the Great North of Scotland 4-4-0 *Gordon Highlander* making a spectacular ascent of the bank with a Stephenson Locomotive Society special from Stranraer to Glasgow in April 1963
Derek Cross

North Eastern Railway: the preserved 'M' class 4-4-0 No. 1621, which participated in the record London-Aberdeen racing run of 1895. This engine, now in the National Railway Museum, hauled the train from York to Newcastle
J. C. Simpson

At the height of Caledonian elegance: the celebrated McIntosh 4-6-0 No. 50, *Sir James Thompson*, built in 1903 and driven by James Grassie with whom the author rode on the footplate in 1934 when he was driving a Midland compound

From a painting by Victor Welch in the author's collection

The preserved Caledonian 'single' No. 123, on a special train. This locomotive is now in the Glasgow Museum of Transport
Derek Cross

OPPOSITE: The preserved Caledonian 0-4-4 tank No. 419, belonging to the Scottish Railway Preservation Society at Stirling, in 1972. This locomotive carries the earlier 'official' dark blue livery
Derek Cross

The 'Caledonian' of the final steam days. The preserved Stanier 'Pacific' No. 46229 *Duchess of Hamilton* carrying the headboard of the fast Glasgow to London express

D. C. Williams

Locos of the North Western main line at Carlisle in 1967: a 'Black Five' 4-6-0 No. 45349 and, behind, a Jubilee, three-cylinder 4-6-0 No. 45562 *Alberta*, waiting to couple on to southbound expresses. *Alberta* was the last of the Jubilees to be withdrawn

Derek Cross

The up 'Midday Scot', descending the
Shap incline at high speed, hauled by
Stainier 'Pacific' locomotive No. 46244
King George VI
Derek Cross

The preserved 'Jubilee' class
three-cylinder 4-6-0 No. 5690 *Leander*,
which has such a distinguished career on
preservation specials, working from
Carnforth
D. C. Williams

The preserved *Flying Scotsman*, temporarily fitted with two tenders for the non-stop Edinburgh-Kings Cross anniversary run in May 1968, here seen leaving Edinburgh Waverley
Derek Cross

In July 1958, the up 'Elizabethan', non-stop from Edinburgh to Kings Cross at an average of 60 mph, approaching Potters Bar, hauled by streamlined 'A4' Pacific No. 60027 *Merlin*. This engine carried a plaque presented by the Naval establishment HMS *Merlin* in Fife, past which the engine ran when working between Edinburgh and Dundee
Derek Cross

OPPOSITE ABOVE: In the majestic scenery of the Lune Gorge, in 1960: 'The Royal Scot' express at high speed prior to the ascent of Shap, hauled by Stanier 'Pacific' No. 46225 *Duchess of Gloucester*
Derek Cross

OPPOSITE BELOW: One of the efficient and much loved 2-8-0s of the Somerset and Dorset Joint Railway, as preserved, and ready for the 150th anniversary 'steam past' at Rainhill in 1980
D. C. Williams

OVERLEAF: The preserved 'A4' Pacific No. 4498 *Sir Nigel Gresley* on exhibition at Carlisle, in 1970
Derek Cross

Britain! It was not surprising that train schedules had to be slowed down, because speed restrictions past the sites where renewal was in progress became frequent.

North of Weaver Junction, 174.3 miles from Euston and the point of divergence of the line to Liverpool, the electrification preliminaries did not yet apply and a brave attempt was made to maintain a reasonable standard of inter-city express service between London and Glasgow. As mentioned in the previous chapter an additional fast train, the Caledonian, was put on in 1957, and then, in 1959, the loading of the 'Royal' and 'Midday Scot's was cut down to eight coaches. With 'Pacific' haulage this limitation in load was intended to provide an ample margin of power in reserve for recovery of time lost by slow running for engineering works south of Crewe, and still to maintain a fast average speed from end to end. As always in the history of the British railways a great deal depended upon the temperament of individual drivers. In this country, unlike France and the USA in steam days, it has never been laid

down as a bounden duty that a driver shall endeavour to make up lost time. Many forms of encouragement have been tried, short always of bonus payments, with varying results. It has never been a case that, as one American running man forcibly expressed it: 'If an engineer don't make up time he goes off the job!'

Before the introduction of limited loads on the daytime Anglo-Scottish trains there was some magnificent running with 'Pacifics' by crews from all the four sheds involved in the service: Camden, Crewe North, Carlisle (Upperby) and Polmadie (Glasgow). On the 'Royal Scot' itself engines worked through between Euston and Glasgow, remanned in both directions at Carlisle, while on the 'Midday Scot' engines were changed at Crewe. Engines and men from Crewe North shed also

At one of the author's favourite photographic sites, a 'Duchess' class 4–6–2 No. 46242 *City of Glasgow* passing Hay Fell, north of Oxenholme, with an express parcels train in 1963   *Derek Cross*

worked through to Perth on some of the night trains. My most vivid recollections of the working of these great engines are from the Carlisle road, over which I was privileged to make a number of journeys on the footplate. I have often felt it was a pity that the full dress trials of the 'Duchess' class engines had to be conducted over the Settle and Carlisle section of the former Midland Railway. While aware of the practical advantages of that route in the lesser density of traffic, the convenience of Durran Hill shed at Carlisle as a base of operation, and the severity and length of some of the intermediate gradients, the 'Duchess' class were essentially *express* engines designed for high-speed work, and it was in this latter capacity that their remarkable qualities were shown, rather than in medium- to slow-speed 'slogging' up very steep gradients.

My own experience of them on the mountain sections of the Lancaster–Carlisle stretch showed the weakness, as well as the strength, of their detail design. Taking for granted the traditionally high quality of British permanent way, locomotive designers in this country have preferred individual rather than compensated suspension, arguing that the latter, although advantageous on a poor road where speeds are not required to be high, tends to induce rolling when the running is fast. The 'Duchess' class 'Pacifics' with individual suspension of all wheels were exceptionally smooth and comfortable riding engines at high speed, though I have known times when compensated springing would have been invaluable for other reasons. While it is of the northbound climb into the mountains – where the line climbs 885 ft in altitude in 31 miles – that my personal memories are sharpest, from my boyhood days in that region, the whole section from Crewe to Carlisle provided a fascinating ground for observing steam locomotives at work, and I shall now tell of six occasions, all but one in the late 1950s, when the work of the 'Duchess' class engines was of absorbing interest. All of them bring out facets of steam locomotive performance that distinguish them markedly from the diesels that took their places. There is no doubt that the Brush Type 4 (B R Class 47) and the English Electric Class '50' put up many brilliant performances in the interim between the last days of steam and electrification; but they never surpassed the maximum efforts of the 'Duchess'.

On four of these occasions I was on the footplate, and so had an intimate view of the tasks the driver and fireman had in hand. On the fifth run, on the morning express from Birmingham to Glasgow and Edinburgh, I was a passenger in the train and logged the running times of a remarkable piece of lost-time recovery, while the sixth was recorded again from the vantage point of the footplate, by my great friend Baron Gérard Vuillet, of Paris, one of the most experienced observers of locomotive performance anywhere in the world. My first run was on The 'Royal Scot' itself, with engine No. 46237 *City of Bristol*, and no more than a moderate load of 415 tons behind the tender; but we were leaving Crewe 10 minutes late and that was a challenge to the engine crew which they took up with vigour. The train was then allowed 163 minutes to cover the 141.1 miles to Carlisle nonstop, not quite so fast as the best time of London and North Western days; but loads were generally lighter in 1916 and earlier. Although we got away from Crewe in tremendous style, and were doing 78 mph in 10 miles from the start, three long and severe slowings for permanent way work and two signal checks prevented us making a better time than $86\frac{1}{2}$ minutes for the 78.3 miles to passing Carnforth. Then, going at 72 mph, the driver opened out for the mountain section and the next 25.9 miles up to Tebay were covered in $24\frac{1}{2}$ minutes, gradients notwithstanding. It was a thrilling experience to go sailing up that dramatic stretch of the Grayrigg bank, where from a high embankment one looks out westward to a panorama of the Lakeland Mountains, at 55 mph. We should have made record time to Shap summit but for a signal check right at the top; but all our late start had been recovered by Tebay, and we rode downhill at no more than moderate speed to reach Carlisle a minute early.

In 1960, when I was a passenger on the 'Birmingham Scotch', permanent way renewal was at its worst and we left Crewe 23 minutes late, again with a load of 415 tons, and the engine the *City of Edinburgh*. This Birmingham train was not one of those subjected to the limited load arrangements and to offset some of the delays experienced daily, its time schedule from Crewe to Carlisle was lengthened to 171 minutes. Even so, with a succession of severe checks we had lost another seven minutes by the time we passed Preston, despite one or two promising bursts of speed. The timing on the mountain section, 31.4 miles from Carnforth up to Shap summit, remained unchanged at 42 minutes, and it was here that we had a really thrilling climb, regaining no less than 11 minutes (30¾ minutes) and averaging more than 60 mph all the way up. The lowest speed on Grayrigg bank was 48½ mph; we dashed over Tebay water troughs at 77 mph and topped the summit, 915 ft above sea-level, at 37 mph – a most exhilarating run to record. I must add that the continuation northwards from Carlisle, with the same engine and crew, was even more so, regaining a further 14 minutes between Carlisle and Beattock summit. It was clearly one of those occasions when everything was going very smoothly on the footplate, and the running data collected from the comfort of a seat in the train gave an accurate assessment of the engine performance.

It was far otherwise on my next trip, on the 'Midday Scot' this time, before the limitation in loading began. As usual the engine came on fresh at Crewe, with a driver and fireman working through to Glasgow, and by the time the through carriages from Plymouth had been added to the train brought down from London we had a 15-coach load, 530 tons behind the tender, on a blustery March evening which turned to thick drizzling rain north of Preston. The engine was a celebrated member of the class No. 46225 *Duchess of Gloucester*, which produced such stalwart uphill power outputs in the dynamometer car trials between Carlisle and Skipton. It was evidently going to be a rough night, and we were lucky not to lose more than two minutes between Crewe and Preston, despite the many times we were slowed down. Then when we got on to the open road north of Preston another hindrance, other than the bad weather, showed itself. The safety valves were blowing off 'light', at 230 lb per sq. in., instead of the rated 250. When these engines did blow off one could lose a lot of steam before the 'pop' safety valves closed again, and this fireman carefully maintained pressure at 208 to 220 lb per sq. in. Despite the bad weather there was no difficulty in wheeling this big train along the level between Preston and Lancaster at 71–2 mph, and we entered upon the mountain section in fine style, passing Carnforth at 70 mph, rushing the first sharp rise to Burton at a minimum of 57 and then rallying to 69 mph before Milnthorpe. Then we struck it!

There was an automatically controlled colour light signal at the location formerly known as Sedgwick, and the warning signal before this was showing yellow. The driver did no more than shut off steam at first. We were by then on a steep rising gradient of 1 in 111, and could stop quickly enough once the brakes were applied; but ahead of us now was the 'home' signal obstinately showing 'red'. In the drizzling rain, carried thickly by the strong wind from the west, the rails had become extremely slippery, and speed was down to no more than two mph before that signal cleared. And when the regulator was opened the engine slipped, and slipped and slipped! In no way it seemed could a grip on the rails be obtained. With this noble machine seemingly impotent we clawed our way ignominiously up the gradient until nearing Oxenholme. There, at a fair-sized shed just south of the junction station, engines were kept primarily for the purpose of assisting heavy trains up Grayrigg bank. In the last years of steam it was rare that passenger trains needed help – it was mostly for freight – but our driver sounded the whistle code that told Oxenholme shed we needed assistance and we stopped just north of the station. Assistance indeed! We had taken 9½ minutes to

In 1963, when diesels were hauling the regular trains, steam was put on to the reliefs. Engine No. 46250 *City of Lichfield* hauling an 'extra' Euston to Glasgow express on the Grayrigg bank, north of Oxenholme *Derek Cross*

struggle up the two miles from Sedgwick automatic signal! A 2–6–4 tank engine buffered up in rear, and we were soon climbing Grayrigg bank in distinctly better style.

All this time however I was wondering how we should fare on Shap itself, with its four miles of 1 in 75 ascent over a fearfully exposed moorland. When we topped Grayrigg summit the bank engine dropped off and on the level stretch through the Lune Gorge we soon attained 66 mph. Then, as if to

In 1964, a Glasgow–Liverpool express south of Tebay, hauled by a 'Jubilee' class 4–6–0 No. 45627 *Sierra Leone* *Derek Cross*

In 1963, when diesels were hauling the regular trains, steam was put on to the reliefs. Engine No. 46250 *City of Lichfield* hauling an 'extra' Euston to Glasgow express on the Grayrigg bank, north of Oxenholme *Derek Cross*

make nonsense of our previous difficulties, the engine took the Shap incline in excellent style, without a sign of slipping. It is true that we had now run into clearer weather, and it was a thrilling, and perhaps poignant, experience to lean out of the cab window, listen to the sharp 'bark' of the exhaust, and reflect that this might be the last time I should ever ride steam up Shap. In the darkness the intermediate colour light signals showed a vivid green beam, and as we drew nearer to each in succession and the signal itself was obscured, from the right-hand side of the cab, by the bulk of the boiler profile, the striking silhouette was set off by the rain of red-hot cinders shooting skywards from the engine's chimney. On the heavy climb speed gradually fell, and the exhaust grew louder until we topped the summit at 22 mph – a memory of steam to carry into the new age.

By comparison, the fourth of my runs to be mentioned was uneventful to the extent that we had fewer delays, and despite a heavy load kept the timing of the 'Birmingham Scotch' easily. Seen from the footplate of the *Duchess of Abercorn* it was quite a model performance, showing, in normal running conditions, an easy competence over a load of 540 tons. The driver was quite an artist in his manipulation of the controls. Whereas some of the drivers with whom I have ridden opened up at Carnforth and let the engine make its own pace afterwards, he, on the *Duchess of Abercorn*, anticipated every change in the gradient, keeping the demands for steam from the boiler practically constant all the way up through the mountains. In contrast, the man who drove the *City of Bristol* opened up hard at the start, when he was doing over 70 mph, and with unchanged controls the demand for steam became progressively less, until he passed Grayrigg summit at 50 mph.

Reference to my own experiences when riding the engines *Duchess of Gloucester* and *Duchess of Abercorn* is a reminder that these two 4–6–2s between them made the British records for maximum ouput of power, in differing circumstances. It was on Sunday, 26 February 1939 that the latter engine, working a special test load of 610 tons from Glasgow to Crewe, topped Beattock summit at a phenomenal 63 mph. The drawbar horsepower as registered in the dynamometer car was 2282, and its equivalent value, related to level track, was 2910 – by far the highest ever claimed for a British steam locomotive. While this tremendous effort, albeit the culmination of a quarter of an hour's

hard pounding, was transient, it was the engine *Duchess of Gloucester* in 1956 that made the record for the highest sustained rate of evaporation in the boiler, at 40,000 lb of steam per hour. This was established in the Rugby stationary testing plant, and verified by dynamometer car tests between Carlisle and Skipton. On a typical ascent of 'The Long Drag' from Settle Junction up to Blea Moor, on a 1 in 100 gradient with a load of 900 tons, the speed was steadily maintained at 30 mph. The drawbar horsepower measured in the dynamometer car was 2000, and the equivalent value about 2300, at a relatively low speed.

One is naturally curious to know how performances under ordinary service conditions, such as those of my own runs over Shap, compare with these monumental occasions. Analysis of the running times on these, and on others made further south on the Liverpool trains, shows that outputs of 1700 to 1800 equivalent drawbar horsepower were fairly common; but it was on Baron Vuillet's run with the *Duchess of Rutland*, in July 1958, that a remarkably high level of performance was attained. A very heavy load of 570 tons was conveyed, and because of many delays in the early stages the train had passed Carnforth $8\frac{1}{2}$ minutes late. The ascent of Grayrigg bank was very fine with an average speed of 39.5 mph over the last 7.1 miles up from Oxenholme, but when it came to Shap it seemed that the driver was determined to show his distinguished visitor a thing or two, and just beyond Tebay, while still going at over 60 mph, he set the point of cut-off in the cylinders at 32 per cent. This was very nearly the same setting that had given that terrific final attack on Beattock in the 1939 trials with the *Duchess of Abercorn*, except that in 1958 the boiler pressure was a little lower; but it gave Baron Vuillet a classic ascent to Shap, with a maximum equivalent drawbar horsepower of 2360. Moreover it was done with very little mortgaging of the steaming capacity of the boiler. The water level was maintained constant, and no more than a slight drop in steam pressure was noted when nearing the summit; and the $5\frac{1}{2}$ miles up from

Tebay (four of which are 1 in 75) were climbed in $7\frac{1}{2}$ minutes.

The institution of limited loads on the day Anglo-Scottish expresses, as previously mentioned in Chapter 2 of this book, had mixed results; but to those crews who really set about the job of regaining lost time the lighter loads gave a chance to make some really spectacular running on the mountain sections. The most astonishing example that ever came to my notice was one very carefully logged by an old friend, on the 'Royal Scot', when that train had been badly delayed south of Lancaster. The engine was the *City of Liverpool* and the load 295 tons behind the tender, little more than half that on Baron Vuillet's trip. With a clear road in the north country Carnforth was passed at 82 mph, and then, believe it or not, the 31.4 miles up to the 915-ft altitude of Shap summit were climbed in $28\frac{1}{4}$ minutes, at an average speed of 67 mph! The going up Grayrigg bank was good enough, with a lowest speed of 57 mph, but as on Baron Vuillet's run the driver would seem to have thrown in all he had on Shap itself; for there, on the 1 in 75 gradient, the speed was sustained at exactly 60 mph. This was a really exceptional effort and involved an equivalent drawbar horsepower of 2600 — not quite up to the *Duchess of Abercorn* record of 1939, but a mighty effort nevertheless.

That figure of speech, 'throwing in all he had', had an amusingly literal echo on one of my footplate runs over Shap. As always when a visitor is privileged to ride on the footplate an inspector is there too. I have always found it very useful. It would not be wise for a visitor to ask questions of the driver when on the run, and an inspector can be a very useful 'guide and philospher'. On one of my trips, when all was going very smoothly, the inspector thought to help the fireman by taking the handbrush and sweeping away the accumulation of coal dust on the shovelling plate just below the firehole door. The fireman had meanwhile been spraying the coal in the tender. When turning round he jogged the inspector's elbow, loosening his already light hold on the brush, which the

strong draught swept from his hand and carried into the firebox! I suppose a strict tally of the fuel consumption on that trip should have read 'x' tons 'y' hundredweights of coal and one handbrush. Actually a 'Duchess' class 4–6–2 working a 500-ton train on 'Royal' or 'Midday Scot' timings would use a ton every 50 minutes.

By 1963 the diesels had taken almost complete possession. Footplate riding had become a white-collar job, and in between other professional duties I was busy studying the working of the English Electric Class 40. I had a pass to ride the locomotive of the 'Midday Scot' through from Euston to Carlisle, but when we arrived at Crewe after a good run down from London we had a leak in one of the water tanks. It was no more than a minor fault in itself, but the locomotive could not continue and a fresh engine was needed at a moment's notice. The locomotive inspector on duty in the station gave us the first thing that was available — not another diesel but a steam 'Pacific', none other than the *Duchess of Rutland*, which had done Baron Vuillet so proud. But that run of his was five years earlier, and in 1963 steam was reduced to filling in the gaps, so to speak. The driver was appalled. By that time steam locomotives were mostly in poor shape, and he said to the platform inspector, 'Don't blame me if we lose a lot of time.' In the meantime someone had gone to find an overall 'slop' to put over my office suit; we all climbed aboard and started away, hopefully non-stop to Carlisle, with a load of 455 tons behind the tender.

We had not gone far, however, before we all realized that the *Duchess of Rutland* was in spanking mechanical condition, and already going like a bomb. Moreover, in utter contrast to every other occasion I have written of in this chapter, we had an absolutely clear road. The permanent way work south of Preston that had caused such chronic delays was then finished, and although the normal heavier loading of the daytime Anglo-Scottish expresses had been restored, the timing had also been quickened by 12 minutes, requiring an overall average from Crewe to Carlisle of 56 mph. I had

Glasgow to Liverpool express in the Lune Gorge,
south of Tebay, in June 1952 hauled by BR standard
class '6P' 4–6–2 No. 72002 *Clan Campbell*   *E. D. Bruton*

Morecambe to Glasgow express climbing the Shap
Incline hauled by 'Jubilee' class 4–6–0 No. 45606
Falkland Islands in July 1961   *Derek Cross*

not ridden on any type of steam locomotive for more than two years, and what a joy it was to be in the old familiar atmosphere again, of coal dust, water spray, the 'sing' of the injector, the smell of warm oil and the compelling rhythmic beat of the exhaust. The engine and her crew took the whole job in their stride. With the clear run through the industrial districts of South Lancashire we slowed, to pass at 10 mph through Preston station, 51 miles in $50\frac{3}{4}$ minutes, and so out on to the grand open road of the north country: 77 mph through Carnforth (78.3 miles in $76\frac{3}{4}$ minutes) and then up the 31.4 miles to Shap summit. The quickened schedule allowed us 39 minutes for this stretch, but we climbed it with relative ease in $35\frac{1}{4}$, and on a merest wisp of steam swept down to Carlisle to arrive in $141\frac{1}{2}$ minutes from Crewe, a gain of $9\frac{1}{2}$ minutes on that *quickened* schedule.

I could write pages of pure nostalgic recollection and technical appreciation of this run; for it was a joyous experience to know that steam locomotives could still put up a superb performance, even though superseded by diesels. This is no place to argue the rights and wrongs of that superseding, but rather to be sure that so far as steam locomotives were concerned 'The Premier Line' of old certainly had machines that were second to none, and on their top form without rivals.

CHAPTER 4
NORTH EASTERN — 'THE MONOPOLIST'

In the 19th century the growth of the railway network in Great Britain followed no ordered plan. There was no neat geographical parcelling out of the country between a few large companies, as in France, no strategic planning as in Imperial Germany; here individual projects were allowed, even encouraged, to develop piecemeal. Anything that suggested a monopoly was frowned upon, and when some financially unstable lines sought to amalgamate with their more prosperous rivals the 'Mother of Parliaments' usually said no. It was all the more surprising, therefore, that the rapidly growing agglomeration of lines north of Leeds and York developed as it did. In the early 1850s the financial situation of the major companies involved was complicated beyond belief. The 'Leeds Northern' was a competitor with the 'York, Newcastle and Berwick', and the 'York and North Midland' had traffic connections with them both. A first proposal to amalgamate met with general disapproval from the three boards of directors, before matters had reached the stage of a parliamentary Bill. But a farsighted plan for traffic pooling and rationalization worked out by the respective managers proved so beneficial that after two years the Bill was presented to Parliament, and in July 1854 it received the Royal Assent. The three amalgamated companies assumed the title of North Eastern Railway.

A very snug monopoly was thereby obtained of the lines lying north of the Humber and east of the Pennines. Two lines striking west across the mountains at first remained independent; but with the absorption of the Newcastle and Carlisle Railway in 1862 and the Stockton and Darlington in 1863 the network was finally consolidated. In the sparse railway literature of the day I had read about the North Eastern before I was into my teens, and from the famous 'F. Moore' series of coloured postcards learned that its engines were green. In the colour printing techniques of the pre-1914 era, however, 'green' could be a very indeterminate colour, and looking through the many cards I now possess I see North Eastern locomotives rendered variously in shades ranging from a dignified blue-grey tint, through bright grass green, to a solemn olive. When I first saw North Eastern locomotives in 1916, I realized that none of these pictorial representations was correct. The passenger engines, all kept incredibly clean for wartime, were decked in a beautiful pale green that could best be described as that of freshly budded leaves in springtime. It did not last very much longer, because in 1923 when the North Eastern Railway became the North Eastern Area of the L N E R, a new colour styled 'apple green' became the standard for passenger engines, and this in its turn was used only on the large 'Atlantic' engines after a few years. Everything else went into black.

But I am writing of the last years of steam in north-eastern England, not of the old North Eastern Railway. The difference nevertheless is not so great as might be imagined. The mechanical engineering legacy bequeathed to its successors by the great company that was formed by the amalgamation of 1854 was a massive one. It was reflected in the longevity of the locomotive stock, greater in proportion to its numbers than that of any other of the old companies whose separate identity vanished in the Grouping of 1923. The longevity, which carried most of its activities through to the last days of steam, was not entirely due to basic excellence in design, nor to any particular favour in which the locomotives were held by the manage-

ment of the enlarged company from 1923 onwards. The new Chief Mechanical Engineer, Herbert N. Gresley (later Sir Nigel Gresley), was a Great Northern man, and while the two companies had, prior to 1923, been staunch allies he had widely differing views on some of the major points of locomotive design. On the L N E R there was however a general policy to allow the existing locomotive stocks of the amalgamated companies to continue in service, and to supersede them only

---

A 2–4–0 'Tennant' class express engine of 1885 No. 1472. This engine made some experimental runs in 1898 with the L N W R dynamometer car, borrowed for the purpose. No. 1463 of this class is preserved
Author's Collection

when traffic requirements were beginning to render them obsolescent. The North Eastern stud was generally in very good shape, and a further reason for allowing the status quo north of York to continue was that very little money was available for replacement in the stringent financial conditions of the 1930s.

It was the experience of the British railways generally that main-line express passenger units deteriorate more rapidly than others, despite careful maintenance, and the conditions of the Second World War certainly took their toll. When nationalization took place in 1948, although more than 1100 steam locomotives of North Eastern design entered national ownership, more than half the original stock of 1923, only forty-seven were passenger engines. This was not really unexpected, in that the old North Eastern was predominantly a freight line, and it was these continuing activities, with locomotives most of which were at least thirty years old at the time of nationalization, that carried on into the last days of steam. At first nationalization made little difference. The North Eastern Area of the L N E R became the North Eastern Region of British Railways, and headquarters remained at York. The old monopoly continued, with the old frontiers remaining the interchange points between one region and another. But then someone with a neat and tidy mind, but not much knowledge of practical railway working, decided that the railway map needed tidying up. It was thought incongruous that the North Eastern Region should have one east–west line extending almost to within sight of western tide-water at the Solway Firth, and another crossing the Pennines and by joint working penetrating into the very heart of the Lake District. New boundary lines were drawn somewhere near the Pennine watershed.

One can understand that some rationalization was overdue in a great centre like Leeds, which in 1948 was entered on their own tracks by trains of the Eastern, London Midland, and North Eastern Regions. Geographically Leeds was North Eastern, and so it became, with the latter taking

over a closely knit maze of London Midland lines, which the L M S had inherited in 1923 variously from the London and North Western, the Midland, and the Lancashire and Yorkshire. These boundary changes did not affect the locomotive working, except that it seemed rather odd that the Anglo-Scottish expresses by the Midland route henceforth passed through territory now lying in the Eastern Region, at Sheffield, and the North Eastern, at Leeds. One example of the new boundary points will make the situation clear. The enlarged North Eastern took in all the local lines around, and extended along the main line to Carlisle as far as Snaygill, an intermediate signal box a few miles short of Skipton; but as far as the Midland Scotch Expresses were concerned it had the important result of bringing the large Midland running shed at Whitehall Junction, Leeds, under North Eastern administration, with eventual results to be described in a subsequent chapter of this book. So far as locomotive working at the end of the steam era was concerned, however, the area covered by the old North Eastern remained virtually unchanged to the last. It was my good fortune to see much of this local working, and to delight in its sturdy character and individualism.

A literary commission in the 1950s brought me into close touch with F. H. Petty, then Motive Power Superintendent of the North Eastern Region. A big, hearty soul, he generated enthusiasm and good humour in all the activities of his department, and so far as I was concerned he would have been quite content for me to spend *weeks*, not occasional days, riding locomotives of all shapes and sizes all over the region. Unfortunately, from that point of view, I had a full-time job of ever-increasing responsibility down in the West Country, and although this, from time to time, involved visits to York and points north when perhaps I could also fit in a footplate ride, for the most part the fieldwork for this particular book had to be done at weekends, preceded and followed by a lengthy night journey from and back to the south-west. With Petty's enthusiastic backing I was able to seek out many of the old

One of the celebrated 'R' class 4–4–0s at Tweedmouth shed in 1932   *O. S. Nock*

North Eastern engines and ride them on duties that had not changed much in some 50 years, though it distressed him not a little that the large express passenger 'Atlantic' engines of the North Eastern had all been scrapped. The last of them went to the breakers' yard in 1949.

Those 'Atlantics', both the two-cylinder 'Vs' and the three-cylinder 'Zs', were among my greatest favourites of pre-Grouping express locomotives. The 'Vs' were inclined to be heavy on coal, but they were massive things and when opened out could pull like a 'Pacific'. I shall always remember the story of a King's Cross fireman, who was on a rather overloaded Great Northern 'Atlantic', arriving at York and having to go forward to Newcastle. He told me how they had a 'V' waiting to couple on ahead of them, and how 'she just lifted us and the train out of York'! The last time I travelled personally behind one of them was at the end of October 1938 when No. 705 was on the

10.05 a.m. down from York, with a load of 310 tons. It was an easy task for a good and powerful engine, and we worked up to a sustained 68 mph on the level at Thirsk. As well as the L N E R style of green painting, those engines had undergone one other change in their appearance from that of thirty years earlier: the form of the safety valves.

In the early 1900s nearly all British locomotives had the celebrated Ramsbottom type of safety valve, a beautifully simple and effective device for preventing excessive steam pressure from developing in the boiler. It was used extensively on a great number of locomotives built in Great Britain for service overseas, and it had been found that the relatively exposed nature of the device enabled it to be 'fiddled', if the driver was so disposed, to get

64

greater than the designed pressure in the boiler, and thus more power. While there was little risk of the highly disciplined British enginemen resorting to such tactics, it became usual to fit a casing round the valves. The larger North Eastern locomotives had a pair of safety valves, and these were encased in a magnificent polished brass mounting no less than two feet in diameter at the top and tapering outwards to its base. Later, when the Ross 'pop' type of safety valve had been invented, to obviate any risk of tampering, these came into general use on newer British locomotives, and the North Eastern 'Atlantics' lost their handsome safety valve mountings when the time came for them to be reboiled.

The twenty 'V' class and fifty 'Z' class 'Atlantics' were all in service when war came in 1939, but with reductions in passenger train services and combining of long-distance expresses into fewer but much heavier trains the usefulness of the 'Atlantics' largely disappeared. Many of them were taken out of service and stored — not very sympathetically it is to be feared! — and by the end of the war they were in a state of decrepitude defying description. I saw some of them on my journeys north in 1945 and 1946, and the sight of those once proud and highly burnished engines was sad beyond words. The difficulty was that accountancy-wise they were still in capital stock, having run far less than their allotted mileage since their last general overhaul; but as traffic machines they were virtually useless. Frank Petty told me how he put the problem personally and confidentially to the regional mechanical engineer. As he put it, 'We got together, and we

Loaded ore train for Consett, leaving Tyne Dock hauled by three-cylinder 0–8–0 (Class T3) No. 63473   *S. E. Teasdale*

Loaded ore train for Consett, climbing the bank from Stella Gill, headed by an '01' class 2–8–0 No. 63856, and a three-cylinder 0–8–0 banking in rear
S. E. Teasdale

scrapped them.' In telling me of this sad end, he went on to talk of the 'Zs' in their prime. I told him of some of my own splendid runs with them in the early 1930s, when they had one or two regular turns on some of the most important Anglo-Scottish expresses; and he rounded off my own recollections of them by saying, 'Yes, they were lovely engines.'

In the 1950s the favours that I asked of him were nearly all on freight trains. The North Eastern had a plethora of short-haul coal runs. Much of the winnings from the Northumberland pits was taken to the nearest port where, from the characteristic high staithes, it was loaded into coastwise shipping. The North Eastern, far more than any other of the pre-Grouping companies, was very preservation minded and conscious of its proud heritage from the first public railway in the world to have steam traction, the Stockton and Darling-ton; its successor, the L N E R, went to considerable trouble and expense to put a brave show of ex-North Eastern locomotives into the Railway Centenary pageant at Darlington in 1925. All the engines that were then restored and took part are still in existence today, and many others have been added, three in particular representing classes that remained in hard revenue-earning service up to the very last days of steam in the north-east. Of all three I have vivid personal recollections. The first is the 'P3' heavy freight 0–6–0, dating back to 1906. As originally built, these massive-looking engines were not superheated; they had a pair of Ramsbottom-type safety valves with the giant encircling cover, like the 'Atlantics', and although painted black had a most impressive look about them. Sir Vincent Raven built another thirty-five of them in 1921, with superheaters and piston valves. It was with one of these more than thirty years later that I made intimate acquaintance.

If one studies a one-inch Ordnance Survey map of 1947 vintage covering the country northwards from Newcastle, the railways leading to the coastal towns of Whitley Bay, Blyth and Newbiggin-by-the-Sea are prominently shown in solid black lines; but a closer inspection of the map reveals a number of faint lines crossed at frequent regular intervals by equally faint strokes, which on reference to the key at the foot of the map indicate a tramway or mineral line. One of these leads down to the narrow neck of land flanking the confluence of the Blyth river and the Sleek Burn opposite to the foreshore of Blyth itself. There is little indication on the map of the activity that once animated this farther shore. For there were ranged the North Blyth staithes, and nearby were the North Eastern running sheds that powered an extensive coal shipping business. Soon after day-break on a cold winter's morning I took a train from Newcastle to Blyth, and the ferry crossing to the north shore gave an excellent foretaste of the icy wind we were to face on the footplate. At the shed the foreman took me out to one of the 'P3' engines that was soon to go out, tender first (!), to fetch a load of coal from Ellington Colliery some eight miles to the north. Tender first on that engine was rather like riding at the front of one of the open-topped buses of old, except that the heap of coal in front of us had to be constantly sprayed to stop dust blowing into our faces.

We took no more than a brake van with us, in which the guard had a warmer ride than we did; and the map shows our route, only 1½ miles of which were over a passenger line. Though the track we took may have been shown on the map as a 'mineral line or tramway' it was in fact a finely maintained double-track railway capable of carry-

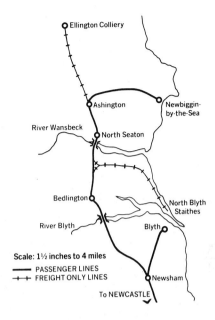

Scale: 1½ inches to 4 miles
—— PASSENGER LINES
+–+ FREIGHT ONLY LINES

ing heavy traffic. Our own engine was no light-weight and scaled nearly 50 tons on its three axles, and when we got to Ellington we found a load of 700 tons awaiting us. There were no facilities for turning an engine at the colliery yard, hence the need to make the outward journey tender first. At the turn of the century the cabs of North Eastern engines were the most comfortable of any in Britain, when running forwards; their roomy side-window shelters gave excellent protection.

I shall always remember a conversation I had when riding another of them southbound from York. After the end of the First World War the large number of 2–8–0 goods engines of Great Central design that had been built for use by the Railway Operating Division of the British Army, in France, were distributed variously among the home railways. They were excellent engines, but compared to those of the North Eastern had a cab that was rather exposed at the sides. On our way south that day we passed one of them, and our own driver and fireman referred to it as one of the 'pneumonia engines'. North Eastern cabs notwithstanding, I must admit to being thoroughly chilled by the time we got back to North Blyth, and I was glad to cross the ferry, snuggle into the warmth of

a non-corridor carriage and get back to Newcastle. The thrill of seeing one of these coal trains being propelled up on to the high staithes could wait for a later visit.

To witness a supreme example of the banking of heavy mineral trains one had to go south of the Tyne. Some 10 miles to the south-west of Newcastle on a hill-top about 800 ft above sea-level were the Consett Iron Works, a strange location one might think for a plant that became one of the largest producers of steel in the north of England; but originally that hill-top was almost solid iron ore. Heavy traffic developed *down* the passenger railway that joined the Anglo-Scottish main line just north of Chester-le-Street. But the mineral traffic did not go on to this latter line. It continued north-eastwards along a purely mineral line that the Ordnance Survey called the 'Pontop and South Shields Branch', but so far as the mineral trains were concerned its destination was Tyne Dock, on the river about 1½ miles east of Jarrow. This great installation was originally concerned with export of coal, but when the iron-ore seams at Consett were exhausted the process had to be reversed and foreign ore imported to keep the great steel works going.

It became the most laborious mineral train 'drag' to be found anywhere in Britain, and it was on this work that I saw, and rode on, the most powerful of all North Eastern freight engines, the 'T3' 0–8–0. The old company had a proud tradition of successful 0–8–0 engine designing, from the Class 'T', introduced as long ago as 1901, to the superheated 'T2' of 1913. Raven was a strong believer in three-cylinder propulsion, like his confrère on the Great Northern; but unlike Gresley he remained a staunch believer in the Stephenson link motion, and his three-cylinder engines all had three separate sets of valve gear. The 'T3' introduced in 1919 was a mighty engine, with a tractive

effort of 36,965 lb, against the 28,800 lb of 'T2'. It was, indeed, greater than that of any of the more modern eight-coupled engines taking part in the Interchange Trials organized by British Railways after nationalization. A mighty engine was certainly needed to get the ore trains of the 1950s up to Consett, and at the end of the steam era all fifteen engines of Class 'T3' (on the L N E R classified as Q7) were stationed at Tyne Dock specially for this job. The standard maximum load was one of 22 hopper wagons, and brake vans representing about 690 tons behind the tender. The trains were banked in rear up the short but steep initial climb from the dock side to Pontop Crossing where the passenger line from Newcastle to Sunderland was intersected; but thenceforward the 'T3' engines were on their own, for nine miles of easy and level road to Stella Gill, just beyond the overbridge across the Anglo-Scottish main line. It is here that the fearful climb up to Consett begins in grim earnest. For the ruling gradient then becomes 1 in 50 interspersed with stretches of 1 in 35 and 1 in 42, much of it complicated by sharp curvature. Another 'T3' buffered up in rear, and after an exchange of whistle signals we were away.

Then, for 35 minutes, I saw a big engine worked as near to absolutely 'all-out' as one was likely to see anywhere. The regulator was full open and the reverser only one notch from full gear, with the valves cutting off steam in the cylinders at 65 per cent of the stroke instead of the maximum of 72 per cent. The roar of the exhaust was music in the ears of a locomotive man, and looking back on the curves I could see from the way the exhaust from the bank engine was shooting skywards from her chimney that she too was being well and truly thrashed. But this was the kind of work for which these engines were designed. Somewhat naturally we were not making any speed records, and on the first stage, to Beamish station, we had been averaging about 11 mph; but 11 mph on a big freight engine going nearly all-out can be as thrilling as 111 mph on an HST, and just beyond Beamish there is a pronounced easing of the gradient, for about half a mile. There was no easing of the

The preserved 'P3' 0–6–0 No. 2392, in full N E R style, near Goathland, on the North Yorkshire Moors Railway   *John Titlow*

locomotives. Both of them were allowed to charge away to nearly 30 mph. The roar of the three-cylinder exhaust was indescribable. And it was just at this moment, when the rate of steaming had been more than doubled, that the safety valves blew off. Still the gauge showed a full glass of water, and it seemed as though this amazing engine could have sustained the effort indefinitely. It is good to know that the pioneer engine of this class (B R 63460), No. 901 of the North Eastern Railway, is now preserved and in the care of the National Railway Museum at York.

As we pounded up those steep gradients from Stella Gill that day we passed near to another remarkable museum, the North of England Open Air, at Beamish, which depicts the past way of life of the country people of the north-east. In the railway area, which has enough track for visitors to be given short footplate rides, there is one of the historic 'C' class N E R 0–6–0 goods engines built in 1889. Even at that early date the elder Worsdell was putting his handsome side-windowed cabs on all main-line locomotives, but I have a special association with and affection for 'C' class. It was on one of these that I rode across the very roof of England in the gathering twilight of a cloudless evening near midsummer. We crossed at

The preserved 'T2' 0–8–0 No. 2238 nearing Pickering with a special from Grosmont, North Yorkshire Moors Railway *David Eatwell*

North Eastern, in 1913: Newcastle to London breakfast car express passing Low Fell, hauled by Class 'Z' No. 735 *R. J. Purves*

Stainmore what is only a few feet short of the highest altitude attained by any English railway, 1370 ft, from which it was a marvellous experience to see the sun going down over a panorama that extended almost to the Solway and the hills of Lowland Scotland. The train was no more than a three-coach 'stopper' from Kirkby Stephen to Darlington, but to ride that little engine was like stepping back into the 19th century, if I had been old enough to do so. Without needing to carry thoughts as far back as that, I have long personal memories of the N E R 'C' class. They began life as two-cylinder compounds on the Worsdell–von Borries system, but it was only below the smokebox doors that a novice would be surprised to see that the two cylinders were of different sizes.

The elder Worsdell, Thomas W., built most of his main-line engines for the North Eastern as compounds, but his younger brother, on succeeding him as Locomotive Superintendent, began converting them to two-cylinder simples. The express engines were done first but most of the 'C' class remained as compounds for many years, and in my first visits to the north-east, from 1916 onwards, I saw several of them still running as such.

So far as cab comfort was concerned I had a most vivid exposition of this one Sunday morning in 1932 when a friend and I were browsing around the little locomotive yard at Penrith. There, alongside, were an ex-L N W R '18-inch' express goods 0–6–0 and an N E R 'C' class. The contrast was extraordinary: the one starkly utilitarian with not a fragment of anything beyond the barest necessities, and the 'C' class with the cab interior handsomely lined with timber, large wooden tool-boxes on either side, and a hooded surround to the fire-hole door. It was more than twenty years later that I rode up from Kirkby Stephen, over Stainmore, and down to Barnard Castle on another engine of the class, old 1609, built at Gateshead 1889 (B R No. 65110), and I found that those big tool boxes were not an entirely unmixed blessing. The space between them was narrow – just enough for the fireman to do his work – and to keep out of his way I had to sit high up on the left-hand box with my legs dangling down in the full heat from the fire. This was during the last years of the railway itself, for regrettably the line over Stainmore has been closed and those marvellously slender and picturesque viaducts at Belah and Deepdale demolished. Some day I must go to Beamish again and have a footplate

Class 'A' 2–4–2 tank engine No. 483 at Tweedmouth Junction sheds in 1933   *O. S. Nock*

ride on their preserved 'C' class, just for old times' sake.

On the day I went up to Consett with the ore train I returned via the steeply graded Derwent Valley line joining the footplate of a two-cylinder 'T2' 0–8–0 at Blackhill for another tender-first ride down to Blaydon. They were great lumbering cart-horses of locomotives, but extremely strong and reliable. I was delighted to learn, a few years ago, that the North Eastern Locomotive Preservation Group had managed to save an engine of this class, No. 2238, from the scrap heap and restore her to full working order for much strenuous work on the North Yorkshire Moors Railway. In easing our way down the sharply graded Derwent Valley line that day, with the tough old 'T2' grinding her way noisily round the curves, we came to Rowlands Gill, deep in this pleasant vale, and I was reminded of a visit there I was privileged to make to J. J. Weatherburn, who had been the inspector in charge of dynamometer car testing on the North Eastern Railway. He was then a very old man, but he had a fund of reminiscence, and delighted in recalling how, with a 'T3' 0–8–0, he had been able to 'wipe the eye' of the Great Western in some maximum load freight engine trials on the Glen-farg bank of the North British instigated by William Whitelaw when Chairman of the latter railway.

Another small-power North Eastern locomotive class that was still very active in the 1950s was the 0–4–4 passenger tank, Class 'O' on the North Eastern and 'G5' on the L N E R. They were first introduced in 1894, and between that date and 1901 a total of 110 were built, all at Darlington Works. All but one of them were still in very active service in 1949, and although withdrawal began soon after, the survivors continued to do sparkling work on the local runs round Newcastle, Sunder-land and Tees-side. On the footplate, one of the delights of a small engine is of an almost perfect lookout ahead, over the top of the boiler, and on an early train from Newcastle we skimmed along merrily towards Sunderland on a route that was once part of the main line to the south. Until 1850,

indeed, the mileage along this line traversed by these through expresses was more than double, because they had to use the awkward layout of the Brockley Whins junctions and reverse direction there, as seen in the accompanying map.

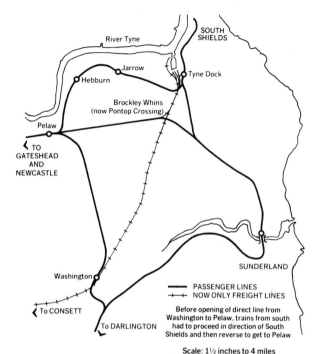

Scale: 1½ inches to 4 miles

Right to the end, these little tank engines were kept in excellent mechanical condition and they glided quietly along like little Rolls-Royces; but at some of the local sheds good mechanical condition was not enough. I was at Bedlington one day, up in Northumberland, when round the curve from the south came an apparition. For one moment I thought it must be a royal special or some other gala occasion; but no, it was merely a little Class 'O' 0–4–4 tank on the 1.09 p.m. local train to Newbiggin-by-the-Sea. In the mid-1950s the pass-enger tank engines at South Blyth shed, as dis-tinct from their freight counterparts at the shed on the north side of the water, were all allocated to regular crews, and I learned that the men were in hot and constant competition as to who could make their engines look the finest. The painting style was then British Railways' lined-black, a close copy of the old London and North Western livery, but this one looked supremely fine. Not only was the paintwork immaculate, but on the five-figure number plate on the smokebox door the background to the figures was painted a deep crimson, and the hinge straps and the surround to the door itself polished bright.

When I had had my fill of footplating on the freight and local passenger train engines I called on Frank Petty to thank him for the many privileges he had arranged for me; but he had one surprise in store. 'What about the "R" class?' he asked. At first I was inclined to demur, suggesting as tactfully as I could that the duties on which those one-time main-line greyhounds were then employed were hardly representative of their past glories. But he waved aside my hesitation, saying, 'Oh, but you *must*,' and immediately began looking through the diagram book to find a suitable train for me. This was easier said than done. About half of the original fifty were still in service, with most of them up at Tweedmouth Junction; but there were still a number of them at Selby, and as these latter took a share in some of the summer Saturday holiday workings to the North Yorkshire coast resorts one of these seemed the most promising bet. Choice fell upon the 11.25 a.m. express from Scarborough to Liverpool via the coastal route. The train was booked to call at Filey and Bridlington, after which it ran to Gascoigne Wood exchange sidings, where haulage was handed over to the London Midland Region. It was not a heavy train in itself, amounting to no more than 270 tons behind the tender; but there were some stiff gradients to be surmounted, both on the coastal section and in the crossing of the wolds between Driffield and Market Weighton. We had a relatively modern 4–4–0 of the 'D49' class coupled ahead of us and this made for relatively light work.

Light work or not, we had not travelled far before I realized why Petty was so anxious for me to have a ride on one of these grand old engines, the particular one being old 1184 (B R No. 62384), built at Gateshead in 1907. Bowling along at 60 mph or so I experienced what I was never fortunate enough to do in their prime — the 'feel' of a North Eastern express engine at speed. It is not enough to say that she rode beautifully, because many good riding engines are rough and uncomfortable to those in their cabs; but this engine was wonderfully smooth and steady, and I could sit down indefinitely. There was no jarring to the body, no jolting, and what little noise there was came from a mild rattle in the cab roof. The engine was then nearly fifty years old, and demoted to a status little more than that of a local train 'hack'; if she was then still so good I fell to imagining what they must have been like in their prime. It is a pity that one of them has not been preserved.

CHAPTER
—5—
EAST COAST 'PACIFICS'

Nationalization of the British railways, in 1948, caught the locomotive department of the former London and North Eastern at an unhappy moment. The five preceding years had been exceedingly difficult. In 1942 Edward Thompson, who had been appointed Chief Mechanical Engineer following the untimely death of Sir Nigel Gresley, gained the general approbation of the locomotive world by his introduction of the 'B1' class mixed traffic 4–6–0. Although the railway world had grown accustomed to all medium and high powered locomotives of the L N E R having three cylinders and the Gresley conjugated gear for driving the piston valves of the middle cylinder, there was logic enough in wartime for building this extremely simple synthesis of existing standard components for general utility service rather than the more elaborate Gresley 'V4' 2–6–2, which was conceived as a general replacement for many ageing medium powered classes in normal peacetime conditions. But when Thompson's drastic reconstruction of the 'P2' class 2–8–2 express engines took place in 1943 the heather was soon well alight.

The reconstruction was bad and ugly enough in itself. But even if one could swallow the argument put forward to justify the work, and accept the resulting 'Pacifics' as a rather hideous wartime makeshift, there seemed no case at all for perpetu-

ating the ungainly wheel spacing as a future standard for both 6 ft 2 in. and 6 ft 8 in. 'Pacifics'. The rebuilding of the 2–8–2s had a distinctly critical reception in the railway press, which was not mollified when the last four of an order for 'V2' 2–6–2 engines of the 'Green Arrow' class were completed, in 1944, as 'Pacifics' with the same wheel spacing as that of the rebuilt 2–8–2s. Thompson himself was very sensitive to criticism, and in 1945 he was becoming increasingly upset by continuing hostile references to further developments in overall plans for modernization of the L N E R locomotive stock; and it was in the late autumn of that year that I became personally involved in the controversy.

To assist me in collecting data for a literary assignment from *The Engineer*, the Locomotive Running Superintendents of the Southern, North Eastern, and Scottish Areas of the L N E R had favoured me with a number of footplate passes. Although these authorities did not come within the responsibilities of the Chief Mechanical Engineer, Thompson became aware of the many and varied journeys I was making, while publication of the earlier articles in the series, dealing with runs on other railways, had commenced in *The Engineer*. The upshot was that before any articles on L N E R running had even been drafted I received a personal invitation from Thompson to visit him in Doncaster. The public relations department at Marylebone, through which senior officers normally made their contacts with the outside world, was taken completely by surprise, still more so when the arrangements for my visit included an invitation to stay the night at his own home. And so, in two hours at his own fireside, he explained to me his reasons for rebuilding the Gresley 2–8–2s, and for adopting as a future standard the peculiar wheel spacing that resulted. He explained also why he was abandoning the use of three-cylinder propulsion in all but the largest engines. He was a charming host, and he pressed his arguments with every evidence of the deepest sincerity.

I shall always remember his opening words: 'Sir Nigel Gresley was one of the greatest engine designers we've ever had; but he made one big mistake.' He then went on to develop the well-known argument against the conjugated gear for driving the piston valves of the inside cylinder. He produced evidence to show me how serious failures had occurred when wear had developed in the pin joints, and how he had set out to eradicate the trouble by using, instead, three sets of valve gear, as had been done on the L M S and in the later three-cylinder engines of the Southern. He told me how he had always admired the four-cylinder engines of the Great Western, because the disposition of the inside and outside cylinders enabled the connecting rods to be made equal, thus resulting in uniform valve events in both sets of cylinders. The conversion of the Gresley 2–8–2 engines, and dividing the drive in the resulting 4–6–2s between the first and second pair of coupled wheels, had enabled him to do the same, though why it should have been necessary to put the bogie so far forward was not made clear to me. Earlier that year I had been to Scotland and ridden on one of the converted 2–8–2 engines from Edinburgh up to Aberdeen. It is not possible to make a true assessment of any locomotive from a single footplate experience, however arduous and varied the traffic assignment may be; but although I had not been particularly impressed with the engine I didn't tell

Thompson so. For one thing the reduced adhesion weight, with three instead of four coupled axles, made the engine susceptible to slipping on a wet rail.

I had not been long in Scotland in that summer of 1945 before I realized how deeply and irrevocably Thompson's policy was dividing the loyalties of all who had to do with locomotives and their running on the L N E R. Before starting away on a footplate run from Edinburgh down to Carlisle I called in to see E. D. Trask, the Locomotive Running Superintendent for Scotland, and in his forthright way he said, 'Now look here, I'm a Gresley man.' Without openly deprecating what Thompson had done to the six 2–8–2 engines, which were then the mainstay of the heaviest traffic on the Aberdeen route, it was not difficult to discern his disapproval. Trask had been trained on the Great Northern, and some twenty years earlier had had the task of taking one of the Gresley 'Pacifics' to Plymouth, on the famous Interchange Trial against the Great Western 'Castles' in 1925. At the end of 1945 Thompson horrified and further antagonized the Gresley faction on the L N E R by rebuilding the very first 'Pacific' No. 4470 *Great Northern* with his own form of front end, cylinder arrangement and ugly wheel spacing, as the alleged prototype of the post-war standard express class. He was very proud of this misshapen, over-elongated engine, and sent me personally a footplate pass for whenever I found it convenient to go.

Had a tape recording been taken of the footplate conversations on that run from King's Cross to Grantham on the down 'Aberdonian' one evening in March 1946, I do not think Thompson would have been very pleased to hear it. The inspector who was deputed to ride with me was also a thoroughgoing Gresley man. He deplored Gresley's early death, and said that if he had lived we would have had more 'A4' 'Pacifics', 'V2' 2–6–2s, and the new 'V4s' of 1941, of which he was a great admirer. Having met Thompson personally, however, I felt very sorry for him: he was a childless widower who lived in a beautiful home, alone, with an old 'nanny' as housekeeper. By one of Gresley's most ardent supporters and a one-time very faithful assistant Thompson's work was castigated as 'pure bloody spite'; but I cannot think it can have been that. It appears to me to have been the work of a man who had an almost fanatical belief in what he thought was right. His cab front was a case in point. The rebuilt *Great Northern* had the square front of the original engine instead of the prow-shape first used on the streamlined 'A4s' and 2–6–2 'Green Arrows', and Thompson was at pains to explain to me why.

While he was Mechanical Engineer of the North Eastern Area of the L N E R, based at Darlington, there was a fatal accident to a locomotive inspector who was riding on the footplate of the up 'Coronation' streamlined express at Wiske Moor troughs, a few miles north of Northallerton. The up and down streamliners were passing at this same point, and the down train taking water overflowed its tender tank. The rush of water hit the engine of the up train, and as both were travelling at about 70 mph the impact was one of some violence, impinging almost at right angles against the inclined front window of the up train engine, smashing the glass and fatally injuring the inspector who was riding just behind the window. Thompson took it up immediately with Sir Nigel Gresley, but no subsequent change was made until he himself was Chief Mechanical Engineer and building new engines. But the inclined front window had a permanent advantage for the footplate men when running at night, as I saw myself on the two stages of that run to York on the 'Aberdonian'. On the rebuilt *Great Northern* the lookout ahead was complicated by reflections in

Greatest days of the Gresley 'A3s': engine No. 2795 *Call Boy* on the down 'Flying Scotsman' awaiting departure in Newcastle Central station

W. B. Greenfield

Austere days, in 1945: a shabby and ill-serviced *Golden Eagle* leaving York with a 17-coach load on the 'Flying Scotsman' with the author on the footplate   *W. Hubert Foster*

the glass of various objects in the cab, lit by the glare from the firedoor. On the streamlined 'A4' to which I changed at Grantham there were no reflections at all in that inclined front window, and the lookout ahead was completely clear.

Thompson discarded another Gresley feature in the only batch of 'Pacific' engines built new during his term of office. These were fifteen engines with 6 ft 2 in. coupled wheels, the first of which, completed in May 1946, was the two thousandth locomotive built at Doncaster Works. These were similar to the converted 2–8–2s of 1943–4, except that in addition to having square cab fronts the Gresley steam collector on the top of the boiler was replaced by a simple steam dome. With the introduction of these engines Thompson felt that his work was done, and at the end of June 1946 he retired. But the company he had served had a

special honour to confer on this sincere and often much misunderstood man, for on 31 May 1946 the first of the new 6 ft 2 in. 'Pacifics', Doncaster's two thousandth, was named *Edward Thompson* at a ceremony at Marylebone station. Only fifteen engines of this particular variety of 'Pacific' were built, because under pressure mainly from the running department his successor made several significant changes in the design for subsequent production. Pressure for change was not entirely from the running department, however, because the new CME, Arthur H. Peppercorn, had been a running man himself in earlier years, and while deputy to Thompson had himself become aware of the vagaries of the latest locomotives.

Thompson left behind him four varieties of 'Pacific', as shown in Table 3. His final gesture to me, on the eve of his retirement, was to send me a photograph of engine No. 500 *Edward Thompson*, autographed, with a request that I would write up the whole process of locomotive standardization on the L N E R that he had set in train. It was subsequently published early in 1947 as a 68-page paperback by the L N E R. By that time the whole railway situation was in the melting pot, with each of the four groups set up in 1923 striving to consolidate their individuality still further before the tide of nationalization engulfed them. On the L N E R Peppercorn took over with an authorization to build a further thirty-five 6 ft 2 in. 'Pacifics', which Thompson expected to be the same as No. 500, his namesake. There was a further authorization for no fewer than thirty-nine additional 6 ft 8 in. 'Pacifics', originally intended to be of the same design as the rebuilt *Great Northern*. Officially no more drawing office work was expected to be necessary, but the undercurrents of opposition to Thompson's policies were flowing fast and deep, not only in the sheds and on the footplate but equally so in the Doncaster drawing office.

Even so, although the record of reliability of the Thompson 'Pacifics' was poor, in all fairness I must add that when in good condition they could put up some extremely fine running. On the down 'Heart of Midlothian' express when I was travelling north one day engine No. 520 *Owen Tudor* took over the haulage at Peterborough of a thirteen-coach train weighing in all 475 tons behind the tender. I rode on the footplate, and recorded a remarkable performance. With this heavy train a speed of 60 mph was attained in no more than three miles of level track, and then the 20.6 miles from Werrington Junction up to Stoke signal box, on an average rising gradient of 1 in 345, were covered at an average speed of 65 mph. The engine rode very smoothly and steamed freely, and generally gave a very favourable impression; but I fancy that it would have been a different story had I ridden the same engine six months later. On the same journey, north of Doncaster, a speed of 75 mph was easily attained on level track, again with comfortable riding. But on track that was less than first class in standards of maintenance the Thompson 'A2s' did not ride well. Flexing of the frames took place between the leading coupled wheels and the cylinders, with cracking, broken fastenings and steam leakage.

On taking over from Thompson, Peppercorn immediately set the Doncaster drawing office on to a redesign of the front end of the 'Pacifics', reverting to a conventional spacing of the bogie ahead of the leading pair of coupled wheels, and the outside cylinders placed further forward. So far as these

Table 3

Class	Number in class	Coupled wheel dia. (ft – in.)	Cylinder dia. (in.)	Grate area (sq. ft)	Boiler pressure (p.s.e.)	Origin
A1	1	6 –8	19	41.25	250	Rebuilt Great Northern
A2/2	6	6 – 2	19	50	225	Rebuilt from 2–8–2
A2/1	4	6 – 2	19	41.25	225	Modified from 2–6–2
A2/3	15	6 – 2	19	50	250	New in 1946

One of the Thompson 'A2' class No. 60519 *Honey Way* climbing the Cockburnspath bank with the up *Heart of Midlothian* train, in 1954   *E. D. Bruton*

were concerned it was a near reversion to the Gresley arrangement, but a separate set of Walschaerts valve gear was provided for the inside cylinder, which drove on to the leading pair of coupled wheels. Two designs were prepared, one with 6 ft 2 in. coupled wheels and a second with 6 ft 8 in., to form the post-war top link express passenger class and ostensibly take over the principal duties from the Gresley 'A4s'. Two details discarded by Thompson were restored on the new engines, the prow-shaped cab front, with inclined windows, and the steam collector on the boiler top instead of the conventional dome. The first of the 6 ft 2 in. engines, classified 'A2/3', was completed at Doncaster just in time to carry the

initials L N E R on its tender, and it was named *A. H. Peppercorn*, after the last CME of the old company. The first of the new 'A1s' was not completed until after nationalization.

The new Railway Executive had barely taken office before the member for Mechanical and Electrical Engineering, R. A. Riddles, had submitted a proposal for a series of locomotive interchange trials. This being approved by the Executive at their meeting on 16 January 1948, plans were rapidly formulated and at first, in the class of express passenger locomotives, there was included 'L N E. Latest 3-cyl. 4–6–2', in other words, the Peppercorn A2/3. These engines had not long been worked in by the time the trials were planned to start; and as on the Eastern Region opinion had then set heavily against any of the Thompson varieties of 'Pacific', reliance had to be placed on the Gresley 'A4s', which of course were then not representative of the latest Doncaster practice. It was ironic, too, that against the generally brilliant record of these engines in pre-war days their unfortunate participation in the 1948 trials seemed to underline all the strictures Thompson had placed upon their basic design. Three total failures on the road, involving considerable delay and provision of substitute engines, told a grievous tale, and one could almost imagine Thompson, in his retirement down in Thanet, saying, 'I told you so!' For those of us with older memories the pre-war record of the Gresley 'Pacifics' was by no means clear of similar failures, some of them highlighted in locomotive history by the positively heroic performances put up by the substitute

engines. So, in 1948, with construction of many new 'Pacifics' authorized and then in progress it seemed likely that the Gresleys would soon be dropping into an inferior place.

There is no doubt that the Peppercorn 6 ft 8 in. 'Pacifics' of Class 'A1', introduced in 1948, were very powerful and potentially efficient loco-motives. They had the internally streamlined front end, which had proved so effective on the Gresley 'A4' class, with the additional advantage of 10-in. diameter piston valves, against 9-in., and the twin-orifice blastpipe and double chimney. They steamed with the utmost freedom, and could readily run up to 100 mph if need be. In addition the design of the machinery was such that they were outstandingly free from incidental troubles, and ran quite exceptional mileages between visits to workshops for periodic repairs. Two factors intervened, however, to prevent these engines

First of the Peppercorn version of the post-war 'A2' class, named after the Chief Mechanical Engineer: No. 525 *A. H. Peppercorn*   *British Railways*

becoming the all-time 'high' of British express
locomotives. Designed for very heavy duty, the
new engines had the same boiler as the reconstruc-
ted 2–8–2, with a firegrate having an area of 50 sq.
ft against the 41.25 sq. ft of the 'A4s'. On anything
less than the heaviest work coal had to be fired
simply to keep the bars covered, and it was soon
found that on comparable work they were considerably heavier coal burners than the 'A4s'.
Then also they were addicted to bad riding. I
personally had one really frightening experience
on the footplate, and even at their best they were
not so easy and comfortable as a Gresley.

The trouble could be traced to the design of the

bogie. On his 'B1' class 4–6–0s of 1942 Thompson
used a very simple bogie with little in the way of
side control. That it differed from Gresley's practice was typical of the day; but while it proved
satisfactory on the 4–6–0s, and its shortcomings
on the various rebuilt 'Pacifics' were to some
extent concealed by the poor riding of the engines
generally, its lack of adequate side control when
used on the Peppercorn 'Pacifics' resulted in their
developing a yawing action at speed. On good
track it was continuous, but not serious or uncomfortable, but on anything less than the best the
'A1s' could be horrible. They would give a sudden
violent lurch, and at other times with the front end
swinging from side to side the cab end would be

lurching six or eight inches from left to right all the time. So, for these and other reasons, when the time came to accelerate the schedules of the long-distance trains reliance was placed once more on the Gresley 'A4' Pacifics. The new Peppercorn 'A1s' were used on the shorter runs such as Newcastle and Grantham, London and Leeds. Peppercorn himself retired at the end of 1949 and was succeeded by J. F. Harrison, again very much a Gresley man; but the revival on the East Coast Route to real pre-war brilliance, and even better, did not begin until after 1951, when in making a general change-round of Regional Chief Mechanical Engineers Riddles transferred Harrison to the London Midland, brought K. J. Cook up from Swindon to Doncaster, and put an ex-North Eastern man, R. A. Smeddle, in at Swindon.

Although Cook had wide-ranging interests in every facet of locomotive working he was above all an outstanding workshop man. On arrival at Doncaster, and taking the measure of the entire 'Pacific' stud, by then no fewer than 202 of them, he found that while the Thompson and Peppercorn varieties were not too well liked for their uncertain riding and higher coal consumption, the Gresleys, both 'A3' and 'A4', were immensely popular, despite their advancing years. Of course Cook, like all senior locomotive men of his generation, was aware of the conjugate valve gear as a potential source of weakness, but there was also the undisputed fact that despite the failures on the road the 'A4s' had come out of the Locomotive Interchange Trials of 1948 with the lowest coal consumption of all the express passenger engines tested. Even before he came to examine workshop practice at Doncaster, the accoustical accompaniment of the goings and comings of the Gresley 'Pacifics' and the other large engines told him of over-generous clearances in pin joints. Some 20 years earlier, when Assistant Locomotive Works

Manager at Swindon, he had been deeply involved in setting up the practice of optically lining up frames, cylinder centre lines and axle centres, which had enabled a high degree of precision to be built into Great Western locomotives.

As a workshop expert himself he was surprised and not a little shocked that the relative inaccuracy of construction methods at Doncaster compelled the use of unusually large clearances in the pin joints of the valve motion. He put it vividly to me once, saying that at Swindon they would scrap when clearances had reached those they started with at Doncaster; but because of the erection

Pacifics of North Eastern and Great Northern design alongside: on left No. 2403 *City of Durham* (ex-N E R) and on right No. 2571 *Sunstar*   *W. J. Reynolds*

methods in use hitherto with the Gresley 'Pacifics' and other large engines those clearances were essential. The process of optical aligning used at Swindon was a German one, and no longer available, but a British system was found and it was eventually installed at Doncaster. The precision in erection that it made possible obviated the need for large clearances in the pin joints, and the three-cylinder Gresley engines with the conjugated motion for the inside cylinder piston valves henceforth ran with the sweetness and silence of a sewing machine, and gave a beautifully accurate distribution of steam. Edward Thompson may have inveighed against the faults and failings of the conjugated gear, but basically there was nothing wrong with it. The trouble lay in the rather old-fashioned workshop practice at Doncaster.

The other mechanical weakness in the Gresley 'Pacifics' had lain in the big-end of the inside cylinder connecting rod. On his large three-cylinder engines Gresley had used the marine type of big-end, whereas on the Great Western an English adaptation of the French de Glehn forked-end type had been standard for inside connecting rods for upwards of 40 years. The form of the

bearing also differed, the Doncaster type being of bronze with whitemetal inserts, while the Swindon had a thin continuous whitemetal bearing, machined to a very high standard of surface finish. Cook's first move was to fit the Swindon type to a number of Gresley 'Pacifics'; it proved very successful, and then, with a view to saving expense, he tried the Swindon type of whitemetal bearing on the marine type of big-end formerly standard at Doncaster, and this was equally successful. Thenceforward, the Gresley 'Pacifics', 'A3s' and 'A4s' alike, attained a reliability in working and in moderate coal consumption that their users had never previously enjoyed, not even in the palmiest days between the two world wars, and the two classes together took their place, undisputedly, as the premier types of the East Coast Route. Cook also put his finger on the cause of the bad riding of the Peppercorn 'Pacifics', namely, the lack of adequate side control on the bogies, and greatly improved them in that respect.

The Peppercorns were highly thought of by the top management of British Railways because of their freedom from casualty and the lengthy mileages they were able to run between visits to works for periodic repair. When the question of new express passenger engines of maximum power was still in abeyance, there was a proposal for a long-term interchange between these engines and the Stanier 'Duchess' class of the L M S: that five engines of each type should be transferred between King's Cross and Camden, and a record kept of their performance in every respect – coal, oil, repair costs; but nothing came of it. At the other end of the line, when E. D. Trask was appointed Motive Power Superintendent of Scottish Region he transferred three Peppercorn 'A1s' to Polmadie shed, Glasgow, for working down the

The Gresley streamlined 'A4' No. 4489 *Dominion of Canada*, on shed at King's Cross, in September 1937 in original condition, before addition of Canadian bell

O. S. Nock

Caledonian line to Carlisle and Crewe. It was before Cook had made the alteration to their bogies, and I shall never forget a footplate run I had on one of them from Carlisle to Symington. It was not at all pleasant!

When the King's Cross–Edinburgh non-stops were reintroduced after the war there was no thought of using any engines other than the Gresley 'A4s'. The Peppercorns would have used far too much coal. It would not have been a case of extending the firemen, because each of them worked for only half the journey, but merely one of carrying capacity on the tender and of getting coal forward towards the end of the run. So it was that the Gresley 'Pacifics' finished their regular careers in a blaze of glory. In the last years of steam the 'Elizabethan' was running the 392.7 miles between King's Cross and Edinburgh in 6½ hours, non-stop, an average speed of just over 60 mph. I was travelling on the southbound train one day when we arrived at King's Cross five minutes early after a series of delays which had cost us about 16 minutes in running, thus leaving a net time of 369 minutes, or a net average speed of 64 mph. The load was the usual one of 11 cars, weighing with passengers and luggage 425 tons behind the tender. The engine was No. 60030 *Golden Fleece*, and the maximum speed 96 mph. A short time afterwards when I was on the footplate of the engine working the 'Tees-Tyne Pullman' express we attained a maximum speed of 103½ mph, the highest I have ever personally recorded on the footplate of a steam locomotive.

Just before the Second World War one of the non-streamlined 'Pacifics' of Class 'A3' was fitted experimentally with the twin-orifice blastpipe double chimney and petticoats in the smokebox in the style of the 'Kylchap' arrangement used in France and adopted by Gresley for the big 2–8–2 engines of Class 'P2', so drastically rebuilt by Edward Thompson. The 'A3' engine No. 60097 *Humorist* remained the only one of the class to be so equipped until K. J. Cook went to Doncaster.

Then, in the course of the routine periodic repairs he fitted the Kylchap exhaust arrangements to all the 'A3s' and their performance was so enhanced that in the last years of steam on the East Coast Route the 'A3s' were being used turn and turn about with the 'A4s' on the principal expresses between King's Cross and Edinburgh, except on the non-stop 'Elizabethan'. In December 1958, when the new diesels were coming into service, I rode on the footplate of an 'A3', No. 60061 *Pretty Polly*, working the 'Flying Scotsman' non-stop from Newcastle to King's Cross. After three severe checks we passed Hatfield, 250.6 miles, in 260½ minutes, 1½ minutes early, and would have been in King's Cross several minutes ahead of time but for some concluding signal delays, and the net time for the 268.3 mile run from Newcastle was 267 minutes.

The engine itself, then numbered 2560, was built at Doncaster in 1925, but it had been so modernized that 33 years later it turned in an impeccable performance. It was indeed the ending of steam on the crack trains of the East Coast Route, because some 10 miles north of York we had passed the northbound 'Flying Scotsman', and that train was hauled by a diesel. As more and more of the new power became available Frank Petty, who is mentioned in Chapter 4 of this book, and who by that time was in charge of all the running sheds in the Leeds area, moved some of the 'A3s' over to the former Midland shed at Whitehall Junction, and put them on to the double home turns between Leeds and Glasgow St Enoch. The saga of the Gresley 'A3' 'Pacifics' as main-line express engines was not yet finished, as I shall have to tell later in this book. But I like to think of my last footplate run on one of them down their own original line and of *Pretty Polly*, riding as elegantly as a dining car, wheeling the heavy 'Flying Scotsman' train along at 84 mph on the level between Thirsk and the approaches to York, and doing a full ninety down the gradient from Stoke Tunnel towards Peterborough.

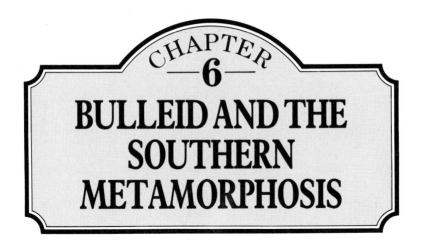

CHAPTER
6
BULLEID AND THE SOUTHERN METAMORPHOSIS

I first became aware of Oliver Bulleid as a power behind the throne on the L N E R about 1930. My friend and one-time boss at Westinghouse, Kenneth H. Leech, then lived in New Barnet, and he had as a relatively near neighbour and sometime travelling companion on the King's Cross suburban trains Bert Spencer, one of the two technical assistants Gresley had on his small headquarters staff at King's Cross. The other was N. Newsome; but considerably senior to both of them was O. V. S. Bulleid, who was personal assistant to Gresley. Nevertheless Spencer, for locomotives, and Newsome, for carriages and wagons, were completely in the confidence of the great man and, through Spencer, Leech learned a good deal of what was happening behind the scenes, particularly as the preliminary designs of all the famous Gresley locomotives took shape on Spencer's drawing board. They were inspired in certain cases and respects by Bulleid, who was a born innovator; but as an assistant his exuberance in that direction was restrained by the massive personality of Gresley. To the end of his time on the L N E R he was no more than 'assistant to—', never Assistant CME, though he came to wield very considerable influence.

He was prominently associated with the more unorthodox of the Gresley developments, especially in the later 1920s with the great compound 4–6–4 No. 10000 with the Yarrow water-tube type marine boiler. He remained closely involved with the running of this locomotive after it had passed beyond the early proving runs and was being used in revenue-earning service. It was largely through Bulleid's venturesome enthusiasm that it was briefly translated from the comparatively innocuous Newcastle–Edinburgh run, with relatively light loads, to the non-stop 'Flying Scotsman'. Bulleid was a strong believer in thrusting the unusual – and experimental – locomotives into the eyes of the running department. In the early 1930s I knew many of the top link drivers at King's Cross and I remember expressing surprise to one of them that the Great Northern 'Atlantic' No. 4419, fitted with a booster, was being used on the London–Leeds Pullman trains. He replied that his colleagues were equally surprised, but that 'Mr Gresley insisted that she was in the link'. I told Kenneth Leech, who in turn referred it to Spencer. It then transpired that it was Bulleid and not Gresley who did the insisting!

When consideration was being given to an eight-coupled express engine to eliminate double-heading on the East Coast main line north of

Edinburgh, Bulleid came significantly into the picture, though always as the discreet back-stage assistant. He had always maintained his French connections. From 1907 he had been Chief Draughtsman and Assistant Works Manager of the French Westinghouse Brake Company, at Freinville, Paris, and he spoke French like a native; from 1930 he was watching the important locomotive developments on the Northern and Orleans Railways, with all the advantage of personal friendship with some of the men closely concerned. Spencer recalled with relish one incident in the preliminary work towards the first 2-8-2 express locomotive on the L N E R. It was decided to make a trial run on the 7.45 a.m. semi-fast from King's Cross to Peterborough with one of the 'P1' freight 2-8-2s normally used on the coal trains. They had coupled wheels of 5 ft 2 in. diameter, and Spencer was instructed to ride on the footplate; but Bulleid urged him: 'Make sure you have an engine standing pilot at Hitchin in case anything goes wrong.' Spencer felt that Bulleid was a good one to urge precautions, having recently lost 30 minutes with No. 10000 on the 'Flying Scotsman'.

Bulleid played an important back-stage part in the detail design of the *Cock o' the North*, particularly in respect of the steam flow and exhaust arrangements, by which no discernible drop in pressure took place between the boiler and the steam chest. He accompanied the engine to France, and was present during all the tests on the stationary plant at Vitry and on the road. It was largely at his instigation – Spencer referred to it as persistent nagging! – that Gresley was persuaded to streamline the 'A4' 'Pacifics' for the Silver Jubilee train. That the great man was not wholly in favour of it could be seen from an incident related by Captain B. H. Peter, Managing Director of the Westinghouse Brake and Signal Company. In 1938, after Bulleid had left for the Southern, the problem of fitting improved brakes to the high speed streamlined trains was becoming urgent; Westinghouse were called into consultation and tests were made with a quick-service application

valve. One day in March 1939 when Captain Peter was with Gresley, a clerk entered the room and handed him a slip of paper. As Gresley read the message a broad smile spread over his face and he tossed the paper across to his visitor, saying, 'There you are, Peter; any of my bloody engines will do the job, whether they have a tin case on or not!'

What had happened was this. On the previous day, when the up 'Coronation' streamliner arrived at Newcastle, the driver's brief examination before continuing non-stop to London revealed a slight defect, of such a kind as to make it unwise to continue. A non-streamlined 'A3' 'Pacific' had been commandeered on the spot, and the 'flyer' left Newcastle eight minutes late. Such was the running made, however, that they were only half-way to London before all that lateness had been recovered: $129\frac{3}{4}$ miles to passing Retford in $120\frac{1}{2}$ minutes. The train was subsequently delayed twice through temporary engineering speed restrictions, losing five minutes; but all save one of those minutes were recovered, and the train was brought into King's Cross only a minute late. The net running time for the 268.3 miles from Newcastle was only 225 minutes, an average of $71\frac{3}{4}$ mph and a gain of 12 minutes on the fast schedule time. No wonder Gresley was pleased, even though this stirring feat was made in retrieving the failure of another of his engines.

Until he was selected to succeed R. E. L. Maunsell as Chief Mechanical Engineer of the Southern, in 1937, Bulleid was little known except in fairly intimate locomotive engineering circles. Indeed, from the time of his appointment as assistant to Gresley, in 1923, there was no mention of him in the influential Tothill Press until his major appointment on the Southern; and *The Railway Gazette* and its associated journals under the management of John Aiton Kay had their ears very close to the ground, taking particular care to keep their readers well informed on what might be called the personalia of the railway industry, both at home and abroad. In other words, in 1937 Bulleid was almost unknown. The choice of him to

succeed Maunsell was undoubtedly made on a conception of future mechanical engineering requirements that proved entirely wrong. Although Sir Herbert Walker himself was on the point of retirement the general policy of development in gradually extending the electrified area was clean-cut, with a continuity and standardization in practice that made big schemes like the Portsmouth Direct, the Mid-Sussex, and the Medway projects little more than routine. Extension of the latter to envelop the whole of Kent was clearly envisaged, and after that there were only Bournemouth, Weymouth and the West of England left.

The lines beyond Salisbury formed such a straggling, unremunerative appendage that there were whispers of handing the whole lot over to the Great Western. What scope would then have remained for the new Chief Mechanical Engineer, other than to act as a caretaker until the existing steam locomotive stock was phased out? As assistant to Gresley, Bulleid had plenty of experience on the carriage and wagon side, and in the perpetual rough riding of the multiple-unit electric stock on the Southern there was ample need for investigation and improvement. Not only this but the foreshadowed electrification farther afield in Kent would require locomotives for the boat trains and continental freight services. All in all there seemed a varied field for the new CME to enter, quite apart from steam locomotives. It is interest-

ing to speculate upon how the motive power situation on the Southern might have turned out had not the crisis of world war burst upon us, for the second time in 25 years. Certain it is, however, that long before the threat of war became a virtual certainty Bulleid's thoughts, far from those of a mere caretaker for the last years of steam, were running towards the production of much larger and more powerful *steam* locomotives.

It is intriguing to try and imagine how, at that particular time, he was able to carry the top management of the Southern Railway with him to the extent of securing the authorization for the plans he was formulating. For when he first went to Waterloo the steam locomotive was regarded as little more than a necessary nuisance. Sir Herbert Walker was still in office at the time of his appointment, though one gathers that it was Gilbert Szlumper who was largely responsible for recommending him, and who succeeded to the General Managership shortly afterwards. In the 22 months that remained before war came, and Szlumper himself left the Southern to become Director-General of Transportation at the War Office, Bulleid's fertile brain was intensely active on various steam locomotive projects. When he took over, the premier express passenger locomotive class of the Southern Railway, the 'Lord Nelson', had a poor record of service reliability, not so much in terms of mechanical failure but of uncertain steaming, which often let the side down with loss of time on the road. To a man like Bulleid, ever ready to leave his office and ride on the footplate, here was a rich field for investigation and improvement. He had no time for the 'King Arthurs', which he considered a crude and outmoded design, but was delighted with the 'Schools'.

But while he at once began an intense and eventually very successful drive to improve the

One of the 'Schools' class 4—4—0s No. 30931 *King's Wimbledon*, with multiple jet blastpipe and large chimney, passing Paddock Wood with a Ramsgate–Dover–London express   *Derek Cross*

'Nelsons' his main thoughts were turning towards much larger engines. Who set the design parameters on which he set to work must remain a mystery for all time; but in 1946 he told the Institution of Mechanical Engineers that he had to design a locomotive that would maintain a 60 mph schedule with the 600-ton Dover and Folkestone boat trains and a 70 mph timing with the Atlantic Coast Express to Exeter. One is curious to know from whom this extraordinary specification emanated. A train of 600 tons made up of standard Southern corridor stock would have involved 19 coaches and have extended far beyond the ends of the main departure platforms at Victoria (Eastern) and Waterloo. It would not only have been a case of extending outwards. With the convergence of other lines beyond the platform ends these lines would have been fouled, and traffic working impeded. One just wonders also how 600-ton boat trains would have been handled at Dover Marine, and still more so in the terribly awkward layout at Folkestone Harbour and its approaches. One begins to gain the impression that the specifi-

cation was one that Bulleid set himself without any real relation to actual traffic requirements.

The care, persistence and skill with which he carried out the improvement and ultimate transformation of the 'Lord Nelsons' was enough to demonstrate his outstanding ability as a locomotive engineer. It was not only a case of altering the draughting. He was sufficiently dissatisfied with the original cylinder and piston valve design to seek and obtain authority to fit entirely new *cylinders*. The veteran designer James Clayton, who had joined the South Eastern and Chatham Railway from the Midland in 1913 as Chief Locomotive Draughtsman, and who had been personal assistant to Maunsell from 1923, had made several

---

Soon after their first introduction, a 'Merchant Navy' class 4–6–2 with original Southern Railway numbering No. 21 C 19 and as yet unnamed, near Hook on up West of England express. The engine was subsequently named *French Line CGT*

M. W. Earley

Holder of the world's record speed with steam traction the 'A4' Pacific *Mallard*, which attained 126 mph on a test run in 1938, here seen hauling the Tees-Tyne Pullman near Potters Bar in July 1959. This engine is now in the National Railway Museum at York
Derek Cross

Not one of Bulleid's favourites(!) but a splendid working design: the preserved 'King Arthur' class 4-6-0 No. 777 *Sir Lamiel*, here seen at Bridgnorth on the Severn Valley Railway
D. C. Williams

A preserved air-smoothed Bulleid 'West Country' 'Pacific' (spam-cans) No. 34092 *City of Wells* on the Cumbrian Mountain Pullman, climbing hard at Horton-in-Ribblesdale in April 1983
David Eatwell

A 'Schools' class three-cylinder 4-4-0 No. 925 *Cheltenham* ready for the 1980 anniversary 'steam past'. The author rode this engine in 1936, on a very fast run from Portsmouth to Waterloo, before that line was electrified
D. C. Williams

The outward-bound Golden Arrow Pullman boat train in April 1960, traversing the series of junctions between the Chatham and South Eastern lines at Petts Wood. The locomotive is one of the 'Merchant Navy' Class, as rebuilt, No. 35015 *Rotterdam Lloyd Line*
Derek Cross

A Deal to London express among the White Cliffs of the Dover-Folkestone Warren, hauled by 'Schools' class 4-4-0 No. 30934 *St Lawrence* in June 1960
Derek Cross

In the New Forest, near Brockenhurst: the northbound 'Pines Express', Bournemouth to Manchester, after its route had been changed from the Somerset and Dorset line to the Southern and Great Western via Basingstoke, Reading and Oxford. The locomotive is a rebuilt Bulleid 'Pacific' No. 34104 *Bere Alston*
Derek Cross

The pioneer British standard mixed traffic engine No. 70000 *Britannia*, now preserved, and here seen running on the Severn Valley Railway near Bewdley
D. C. Williams

In the picturesque Sonning Cutting, in September 1960: one of the Welsh-based 'Kings', No. 6009 *King Charles II* on a Fishguard to Paddington express
Derek Cross

On the sea wall at Dawlish in September 1959, a Wolverhampton to Penzance express, hauled by engine No. 5025 *Chirk Castle*
Derek Cross

At Newport (Mon.) crossing the Usk viaduct: the preserved No. 6000 *King George V* hauling a special train
D. C. Williams

In July 1983, the preserved 'Castle' class 4-6-0 No. 5051 *Earl Bathurst* leaving Hereford for the north
David Eatwell

OPPOSITE ABOVE: 'The William Shakespeare', charter train on 6 June 1983 hauled by the *King George V* in Harbury Cutting south of Leamington
David Eatwell

OPPOSITE BELOW: On the Severn Valley Railway: the preserved 4-6-0 No. 4930 *Hagley Hall*, hauling the Great Western Society's vintage train to Bridgnorth
D. C. Williams

In the depths of Sonning Cutting: engine No. 5032 *Usk Castle* passing beneath the Bath Road bridge, with an express for Bristol and Weston-super-Mare
Derek Cross

The preserved 'Black Five' 4-6-0 No. 5000, the class leader, at Crewe Bank Sidings, Shrewsbury
D. C. Williams

Before the end of steam: a 'Black Five' No. 45296 toiling up the Shap incline, with a Morecambe to Glasgow excursion in 1964
Derek Cross

attempts to improve the steaming of the 'Lord Nelsons', including a reversion to the conventional arrangement of crank axles, giving four instead of eight exhausts per revolution, on one engine, and the Kylchap form of twin-orifice blastpipe and double chimney on another; but Bulleid went through no fewer than nine stages of development before he arrived at the final form of multiple jet blastpipe. Its success was astonishing and gave Bulleid the data he needed for the all-important exhaust arrangements for his new 'super' main-line locomotive. Clayton's health was failing, and although he was persuaded to remain in office for a year as personal assistant to Bulleid he took little part in the new work. It has, indeed, been suggested that he was very much out of his depth.

Bulleid would very much have liked to build his new engine as a 2–8–2. As the author of many of the unusual features of the L N E R *Cock o' the North* he had a natural partiality to the wheel arrangement, which contrary to opinions sometimes expressed elsewhere had proved very successful on the Edinburgh–Aberdeen section of the East Coast main line. But in putting forward the 2–8–2 he immediately came into conflict with the Chief Civil Engineer of the Southern, the timorous and very touchy George Ellson. In his younger days Ellson had the reputation of being something of a bully, though his attitude to fellow officers, and particularly to contractors, mellowed considerably when in the presence of the great A. W. Szlumper, Chief Engineer of the Southern and father of the new General Manager. But Ellson had not long succeeded Szlumper when there occurred the disastrous accident near Sevenoaks when, partly due to poor riding qualities and partly due to bad track, a 2–6–4 express tank engine left the road at a speed of about 60 mph and many lives were lost. Ellson had a nervous breakdown in consequence, and although he recovered, to remain many years in office as Chief Engineer, he always had a thing about engines with leading pony trucks, and even before Bulleid arrived on the scene he had vetoed a proposal for a 'Pacific' version of the 'Lord Nelson', on account of weight.

Bulleid, however, was a master in all metallurgical matters, and when his great, mysteriously encased 'Merchant Navy' class 'Pacific' appeared in 1941 it was revealed that he had produced an engine having a tractive effort of 37,500 lb, with an all-up engine weight of only 94¾ tons. This compared with 105¼ tons for the L M S 'Coronations' (after the streamlining had been removed) and 103 tons for a Gresley 'A4' 'Pacific', the tractive efforts of which were 40,000 and 35,455 lb respectively. The weight per pound of tractive effort in the three cases was 5.67, 5.9 and 6.53 for the Southern, L M S and L N E locomotives. Beyond the fact that Bulleid's engine had unusually small cylinders, very high boiler pressure and an unorthodox form of valve gear, little was vouchsafed at the time. Some critics wondered, if there had been so evident a need to keep the weight down, why it should have been externally streamlined – or air-smoothed as it was called at the time. But Bulleid was nothing if not a showman, and that casing heightened the interest and deepened the mystery as to what was inside. Rumours soon began to circulate about failures on the road, plentifully exaggerated by those who sought to deprecate anything produced on the Southern; but it was not long before the ten engines of the class were generally accepted as a notable contribution to the national war effort, skilfully contrived publicity-wise in that one of the very first photographs of one of them in service was on a heavy freight train.

By the time VE Day came, on 8 May 1945, construction of the second batch of these engines was well advanced at Eastleigh, while Brighton was almost ready to out-shop the first of the smaller and lighter 'West Country' class. It was at that time too that I became personally associated with Bulleid through an introduction arranged by John Kay of *The Railway Gazette*. My great friend, the late W. J. ('Josh') Reynolds, was in the editorial department of Longmans, Green and Co. He was one of the finest 'portrait' photographers of solo locomotives I have ever known, and he was very anxious that the series of articles I had contributed

An early picture of a Bulleid 'Pacific' No. 35029. The nameplates are fixed, but covered over pending the official naming ceremony. The name was *Ellerman Lines*   *E. D. Bruton*

to *The Railway Magazine* in 1941–3 on 'The Locomotives of Sir Nigel Gresley' should be published in book form with very many more photographs. He was the principal architect of an agreement between John Kay and Longmans to do this, and he designed the book himself. Kay had the idea of getting Bulleid to write a foreword to the book, introduced me to him, and 'O.V.S.B'. did it very charmingly. That was early in 1945, and as soon as VE Day had come and gone he arranged for me to ride on some of his own engines. And so in the late summer of that year I sampled the footplate working of three different 'Merchant Navys' and one of the brand new 'West Country' 'Pacifics'. That they gave very mixed results, even at that early stage, was typical of the breed as a whole; and it was before the Institution of Mechanical Engineers in December 1945 that Bulleid himself laid bare the

innermost details of the design in a monumental paper modestly titled 'Some Notes on the "Merchant Navy" class Locomotives, Southern Railway'.

In the discussion on this paper T. Henry Turner, the distinguished metallurgist of the L N E R, said: 'The "Merchant Navy" locomotives stand out from their background, they stand out at the head of trains, and they stand out as leaders of thought. To railwaymen, "Pacific" main-line locomotives are more than engines; they resemble the banner, or the band, at the head of a procession; they give direction and pride and comradeship to the whole of the railway staff. The author has raised a new banner. There is still novelty in the steam locomotive. When one looks across the lecture theatre to the portrait of the author's old chief, Sir Nigel Gresley, who also designed and wrote papers about locomotives, one feels that Sir Nigel would have wished to join the members present in congratulating the author on an outstanding paper.'

In the entire history of the steam locomotive a truer phrase was never uttered than that of Turner: 'they give direction and pride and comradeship to the whole of the railway staff'. The Bulleid 'Pacifics' did just that. When party politicians, for their own ends, talked about the British railways being a very poor bag of assets the men of the Southern were rising to the very crest of the

Engine No. 35016 *Elders Fyffes* (Merchant Navy class) on the 'Devon Belle' all-Pullman express passing Raynes Park   *Ian S. Pearsall*

wave, proud beyond measure of their spectacular new engines and ready for the opportunity that came in 1948 of going out to 'lick the pants off' all rivals. While the Southern stood by to cheer, others derided the 'spam-cans', as the air-smoothed 'Pacifics' were dubbed. I shall always remember an altercation between two of my railway friends over tea at the Institution of Mechanical Engineers before a meeting. One was waxing almost lyrical over the virtues of the 'Merchant Navys': 'They're marvellous,' he exclaimed. 'They'll steam on anything – garden refuse, egg shells, anything you like to chuck in!' 'Fair enough, old boy,' the other cut in. 'But you've got it the wrong way round. Build your bonfire by all means, but then put the b— engine on top of it!'

At their best the Bulleid 'Pacifics' were magnificently strong and free-running engines. Their outstanding feature was the boiler, which was designed to deal with the worst possible grades of coal and did so triumphantly well. It was assisted by the draughting arrangements, including the multiple jet blastpipe and very large diameter chimney which Bulleid had developed to near-perfection in his rehabilitation of the 'Lord Nelson' class 4–6–0. Having said that, however, I come to what I think is the most extraordinary part of the 'Pacific' engine saga on the Southern Railway. In 1945 there were ten of the 'Merchant Navy' class in service, and another ten in course of construction. The teething trouble, which was really the most polite thing one could call it, was by no means resolved, and yet at this time the Board authorized the construction of no fewer than seventy of the smaller 'West Country' class – *seventy*! True, this remarkable building programme was to be spread over nearly two years, but was such an enormous fleet of 'Pacifics' really necessary? It was intended that they would be the standard replacement for a variety of ageing medium powered engines that the Southern had inherited in 1923, variously from the London and South Western, the Brighton, and the South Eastern and Chatham Railways.

Before considering the impact, or more correctly the lack of impact, of this astonishing building programme it is necessary to examine the central and most critical feature of the whole design, the valve gear. Bulleid's predecessor as Chief Mechanical Engineer of the Southern, R. E. L. Maunsell, followed in the tradition established by Robert Urie, when he succeeded Dugald Drummond as CME of the London and South Western Railway in 1912: 'Make everything get-at-able.' In designing the 'Merchant Navy' class and the smaller 'West Countrys' Bulleid followed a totally different philosophy, one more akin to automobile practice. In the attention it needed when on shed the steam locomotive was labour-intensive, and for more than a hundred years it had been taken for granted that it was so. But by the 1940s there were stirrings away from those time-honoured traditions. Elsewhere in Great Britain self-cleaning smokeboxes were being introduced, which were intended to obviate any need for opening the smokebox door from one boiler washout day to the next – sometimes up to ten days. Bulleid turned his attention to the valve gear in the hope of making it immune from any need of attention for far longer periods than ten days. As assistant to Sir Nigel Gresley he had had his fill of experience with three-cylinder locomotives and the troubles that beset the big-end of the inside cylinder connecting rod, and he designed something entirely different.

A three-cylinder engine, with the relatively light pistons and rods, enabled him to dispense with any form of reciprocating balance weights, and he put the inside 'engine', including the connecting rod and crank axle, and the entire valve gear into a closed compartment containing an oil bath. The mechanism would be continuously and generously lubricated, and other than periodic topping up with oil the entire motion would run for months without attention. The whole conception was so absolutely *right* that its successful application to a hard and intensively used locomotive promised as major a breakthrough in the advancement of steam locomotive practice as any seen since the introduction of long-lap, long-travel piston valves, and the internal streamlining of the steam passages and valve ports. It would, however, not need a great deal of intimate and expert knowledge of the design of the machinery of locomotives, and the severe treatment it had to withstand in the ordinary course of fast express running, to appreciate that such a project would introduce many factors hitherto unknown. Those concerned with automobile practice often find almost beyond belief the vibration that is imparted to the motion of a locomotive with a steel wheel running over steel rails; and successful valve gear, piston and connecting rod design had been gradually evolved from the experience with ever larger and faster running locomotives.

The design of a totally enclosed inside motion

The now-preserved 'West Country' Pacific No. 34092 *City of Wells*, working the Cumbrian Mountain Express across Arten Gill viaduct on the Settle and Carlisle line, in 1982　　　　*David Eatwell*

was the kind of challenge in which Bulleid revelled. Much of it was his personal work. In the long history of the British steam locomotive many famous designs are credited to those who were heads of the department at the time, when in a majority of instances the Chief laid down little more than the broadest requirements, leaving everything else to his drawing office or to the contractors entrusted with the building of the locomotives. But Bulleid's involvement with the 'Merchant Navy' class was absolute, to the distraction, not infrequently, of his chief draughtsman at Brighton Works where the detail design was worked out. In propounding so novel a feature as that totally enclosed motion a cautious and more prudent approach would have seemed to be the building of one or two prototype boxes that could be subjected to exhaustive testing, with the remaining engines of that first batch of ten fitted with an orthodox valve gear. That, however, was not to know the nature of Oliver Bulleid. The new valve gear must be fitted on them all, at once; not only so but the second lot built in 1945 were the same, and so also were the 70 smaller engines of the 'West Country' class. It proved the death-knell of the Bulleid 'Pacifics' in their original form.

While in the long term these engines were a big disappointment from the technological point of view, one nevertheless cannot over-emphasize the tremendous boost they gave to everyone concerned with train running on the Southern in the years just after the war. The nation as a whole was sick and tired of making do with privations and austerity. Everyone was yearning for a new look, and Bulleid gave it to his railway. Furthermore the engine crews quickly found that the new locomotives were immensely powerful and, though there were some failures, in general the men were delighted. Bulleid carried everyone along with

The second of the 'Schools' class, No. 30901 *Winchester*, with Bulleid modifications of the blast-pipe and chimney, on London to Brighton train at Oxted, in June 1959   *Derek Cross*

him. His design staff tore their hair at times, but there was no restraining him. 'If he'd asked for square wheels,' one of them exclaimed, 'we'd have given them to him.' In parenthesis one might whisper that it would have been more than their life was worth not to do so. The bosses of the running department who had to take responsibility for the use of the engines in traffic were not so enthusiastic, but lower down the chain of command Bulleid never had more wholehearted support than from J. Pelham Maitland, the Shed Superintendent at Nine Elms. His engines had to carry the banner of the Southern into the arena of the 1948 Interchange Trials, and in that event it would not be far short of the mark to say that they won undying fame.

Maitland chose the enginemen personally, and briefed them in such a way that they went out in a spirit of boundless enthusiasm. In the Grouping era, when the L M S and the L N E R were rising to such heights of engine performance, the steam men of the Southern were resigned to their eventual superseding by the multiple-unit electrics; but in 1948, thanks to Bulleid, they were able to go out at least as equals of the products of the great Gresley and Stanier traditions. Before the contest was finished they had registered the highest recorded values of 'equivalent drawbar horsepower' of any engines, in both the express passenger and the mixed traffic classes. The 'West Country' engines in particular put up some astounding performances and the record of 2010 e.d.h.p. by No. 34006 *Bude*, on one of the southbound runs over the Great Central line, was the highest of any noted in the official report on the trials. Despite the tendency of the inside valve gear to give trouble, the Bulleid engines came through the trials with a completely clean bill of health, which was more than could be said of some of their competitors. As a result of these trials the

One of the Bulleid air-smoothed 4–6–2s No. 34106, at that time unnamed, on Plymouth to Brighton express at Seaton Junction, in September 1959   *Derek Cross*

Southern locomotive department was elated, and its many amateur supporters likewise, even though the coal consumption of the Bulleid 'Pacifics', as revealed by the published report on the trials issued in 1949, was shown to be heavier than those of all their competitors. But high coal consumption never worried Bulleid. He always said it showed that his engines were doing a lot of hard work. And so they undoubtedly were.

Much as he personally disagreed with the policies being developed on the nationalized British Railways, Bulleid remained completely loyal to the 'Centre'. Men who attended the top level committees on which he served have told me that never did he attempt to rock the boat; but any influence he may have had with the new regime ceased abruptly when he retired at the end of September 1949. After he had gone to Ireland and there had been a general change round of the regional mechanical and electrical engineers, one of the 'Merchant Navy' class was sent to Rugby for examination on the stationary test plant to establish, to quote from the official report, 'data directly applicable to the immediate commercial purpose of examining train loadings and schedules to obtain reduction in fuel consumption by working the locomotives, where possible, nearest their point of maximum operating efficiency'. Bulleid's biographer, Sean Day Lewis, has suggested that the locomotive in question, No. 35022 *Holland Amerika Line*, assumed the human traits so often attributed to the species *genus locomotivicus*, and aped her designer, regarding the whole process to which she was submitted at Rugby as so much pedantic nonsense, and accordingly led the testing staff one hell of a dance.

The measured phraseology of some parts of the official report does not entirely gloss over the adventures they had in trying to make this highly unorthodox locomotive conform to traditional methods of testing. I knew some of the engineers involved, and their stories would make a book of their own. The adventures had reached no more than a half-time stage when the engine left Rugby and was sent to Carlisle for road testing with the dynamometer car between there and Skipton. I have always felt that the results of these tests were prejudiced by comparison with the brilliant results obtained in the 1948 Interchange Trials as the locomotive was driven and fired by local men instead of by the enthusiastic Southern crews who did so well earlier. But of course on British Railways standardization was the order of the day, and anything that did not conform was immediately suspect. Failures on the road there certainly were from the totally enclosed valve gear, and the official report on the Rugby and road trials condemned the engines on the grounds of excessive coal consumption; but from the traffic working point of view one of their greatest disadvantages was the liability to persistent and at times almost uncontrollable slipping.

By their many staunch supporters it was often pointed out that this trait was hardly, if at all, evident during the 1948 Interchange Trials; but during the progress of that event the Southern engines were handled by expert drivers personally selected by J. Pelham Maitland. It was when the engines came into general use, particularly the large numbers of the smaller 'West Country' and 'Battle of Britain' classes, that this disability became something of an embarrassment. On certain routes it led to the fixing of load limits considerably below the tonnages that would have been expected for locomotives having a nominal tractive effort of 31,500 lb. One of the first B R steps towards modifying the Bulleid 'Pacifics' was to reduce the boiler pressure on both classes to 250 lb per sq. in. and in the mid-1950s the tide of evidence against the economic value of the Bulleid 'Pacifics' mounted. At one time there was even a suggestion that they should all be scrapped. With the launching of the modernization plan for British Railways, the prospect that the north-going lines would have many relatively new steam locomotives surplus to requirements lent some weight to these thoughts. It was soon evident, however, that despite the urgings of the non-technical anti-steam faction at British Railways headquarters the revolution in motive power was going to be some time in coming, and so far as the Bulleid 'Pacifics' were concerned the project of scrapping was passed over in favour of rebuilding on more orthodox lines.

In February 1956 engine No. 35018 *British India Line* was out-shopped from Eastleigh Works in a new guise. The air-smoothed outer casing had been removed, together with the original inside gear and the oil bath. New outside cylinders were fitted, and three sets of conventional Walschaerts valve gear applied. All thirty of the 'Merchant Navy' class were similarly altered afterwards, and sixty out of the 110 smaller 'Pacifics'. The work of rebuilding the 'Merchant Navy' class went on until October 1959, while the last 'West Country' to be so treated was not back in traffic until June 1961. The second engine to be altered, No. 35020 *Bibby Line*, was put through a series of full dress trials using the Swindon dynamometer car but, far from trying to emulate Bulleid's ambitious performance specification, in the service trials on the Atlantic Coast Express the traffic department reduced the normal load of the train by one coach to compensate for the inclusion of the dynamometer car in the load to be hauled. In traffic they became rather respectably reliable. Sean Day Lewis in his biography put it more succinctly: 'They had also lost the features which gave them their mystery and panache, which made them an engine apart, brilliant and mercurial, as independent and unpredictable as their designer.'

This is not to say that they ceased to perform hard and speedy running on the line; but most of the express drivers would agree that they were neither so fast nor so powerful as of old. The erratic behaviour of the chain-driven totally enclosed valve gear, which gave the boffins of the Rugby testing station such a perplexing and frustrating time, could sponsor prodigious outputs of power on the road, while of course the reduction in the boiler pressure did not help. Nevertheless in their last years the Southern 'Pacifics' of both large and small varieties continued to do good work, while in 1962 a maximum speed of 104 mph was recorded near Axminster with engine No. 35028 *Clan Line*, while working the down Atlantic Coast Express. This engine is now preserved in full working order and used for hauling steam specials. In the last week of steam traction on the Bournemouth route, in the summer of 1967, when enthusiasts were travelling specially to secure their final experiences, some of the drivers entered into the spirit of the occasion and pressed their engines to feats of high speed, particularly on the favourable stretch eastbound from Basingstoke. In that last week a maximum speed of 103 mph was claimed for No. 35003 *Royal Mail*, and of 97 mph for the 'West Country' No. 34021 *Dartmoor*; but I just wonder how much higher speeds might have been attained with engines having the original Bulleid valve gear.

CHAPTER 7

THE 'BRITANNIAS'

Few of us who had any regard for the old private railways of Great Britain and for those who ran them, and who appreciated the inestimable services they had given to the nation in more than a hundred years, relished the prospect of nationalization, following the General Election of 1945. Realizing, however, that it would be the dedicated railwaymen of the old companies who would have to effect the change – not the perfervid politicians who had framed the Labour Party's Election Manifesto and steamrollered the Bill through Parliament – most of us looked with sympathy and not a little anxiety as to how things would work out. And so this chapter inevitably becomes involved with the policies adopted by those saddled with the responsibility for mechanical and electrical engineering.

This is no place to try and analyse the technical rights and wrongs of what was attempted from 1948 onwards. Of course, to the layman interested in railways the designing and building of locomotives may have seemed the predominant task – if not entirely the only one – of a Chief Mechanical Engineer, but as my great friend, the late Roland C. Bond, wrote in his autobiography (*A Lifetime with Locomotives*): 'They were only one among a host of matters involved in the direction and management of a department with 100,000 men, spending £100 million a year, and responsible for

all the mechanical and electrical engineering activities of British Railways.' But for good or ill, the attention of everyone concerned with locomotives, the regional railway establishments, the manufacturing industry, the technical press, and the great body of amateur enthusiasts were alike agog to see what the new all-L M S triumvirate were going to do about motive power for the nationalized railways.

From the policy of locomotive standardization established in Stanier's time there was indeed an L M S design that could well have been adopted as a national standard in all except two categories of service. Those exceptions were a high-power mixed traffic class, and a freight engine of larger capacity than the generally popular 2–8–0. Of the former, there were two existing designs that might have been considered: the Gresley 'V2' 2–6–2, which had a notable record of service to its credit, despite the anti-Gresley propaganda waged on the L N E R during the latter part of the war, and the Bulleid 'West Country' 'Pacific' of the Southern, which had put on some outstanding performances during the 1948 Interchange Trials. Both classes had 6 ft 2 in. coupled wheels, and the nominal tractive efforts were 33,730 lb (V2) and 27,715 lb (WC). Both had three cylinders, but both had valve gears that were not acceptable to the 'powers that were' at Railway Executive headquarters. How

the ex-L M S triumvirate, R. A. Riddles, Roland C.
Bond and E. S. Cox, determined upon the difficult
course of designing an entirely new range of locomotives that should be a synthesis of all that was
best in the regional types has been described and
discussed at great length by other pens than mine.
Here I am offering no more than a few anecdotes
and reminiscences of what can only be called a
rather chequered phase of British locomotive
history.

Looking back rather more than 30 years, when
the first of the 'Britannia' class 'Pacifics' was first
put into traffic, I can now feel rather sorry for those
who then held the ultimate responsibility; for
taking the most charitable view of it they did not
get off to a very good start. All eyes were upon
them, and the news of their early failures spread
like wildfire. Some of the troubles stemmed from a
quixotic altruism on the part of the Railway
Executive to make the new engines a synthesis of
all that was best in the regional design practices.
The principle was carried further, in that the
regional headquarters drawing offices of Brighton,
Derby, Doncaster and Swindon were each allo-

110

cated certain features of the design, not only of the 'Britannia' 4–6–2s but of the entire new range of standard locomotives. Cox, as Executive Officer, Design, was the central co-ordinating hand in carrying out the detail allocations decided at Railway Executive headquarters, and it must be admitted that he was saddled with a very difficult and at times delicate task. That within the overall remit choices of many individual items of detail were his own is evident from his various writings and technical papers; but in the cold light of history it cannot be said that the 'Britannias' were conspicuously successful or well-liked engines.

Having said that, I must immediately add that in one area, East Anglia, their success was in every way absolute. A major proportion of the first batch of 25 engines, built in 1951, was allocated to Stratford and Norwich sheds; and when further engines of the class had been built in the following year the allocation to the Great Eastern line was made up to 23, of which 13 were stationed at

Stratford and 10 at Norwich. Never previously in that area had engines of such size and power been available, and all concerned made a particular effort to ensure they were used to the best advantage. In a compact geographical area all the workings were closely regulated, and on the majority of the daily diagrams the engines were double-shifted, in certain cases working mileages in excess of 450 a day. There were nine daily diagrams from Stratford, averaging 415 miles each, while the seven Norwich diagrams averaged 364 miles each. These regular workings which included goods as well as express passenger duties left a balance of four engines spare at Stratford and three at Norwich, an adequate margin for engines under repair, and shed days. Well maintained, the

Summer Saturday on the Western Region: a relief express Paignton and Torquay to Paddington climbing the Bruton bank, hauled by 4–6–2 No. 70020 *Mercury*   *Ivo Peters*

111

'Britannias' became well liked by all concerned with their use in East Anglia.

Elsewhere it was otherwise. The remaining 32 engines of the class were distributed between the London Midland, Scottish, Southern, and Western Regions, on all of which it was expected that they would take over the duties hitherto performed by the Class '7' express passenger 4–6–0s. But the allocation was sparse and it cannot be said that the new engines received a particularly enthusiastic welcome anywhere. Except in two cases the relatively few engines of the class available precluded any careful grouping into closely observed diagrams, and the engines became common user. Of course this was part of the philosophy behind the design itself; but the individual features and peculiarities of the new engines, contrasting with the well-known and much appreciated regional types, militated against their success as isolated units among all others. The two exceptions to this otherwise indiscriminate use were the small group of 'Britannias' at Canton shed, Cardiff, used on the South Wales to London expresses, and an even smaller group at Holyhead, which took over the workings of the Irish Mails to and from Euston. The Holyhead group, which involved the longest continuous working ever regularly operated by these engines, of 263 miles 'double-home' for both engines and men, did not entail any daily mileages approaching those regularly worked in East Anglia.

In the first few years of their service, when the engineers of the Railway Executive believed that steam traction would continue to play a major part in British railway operation for many years to come, I rode about 1,500 miles on the footplates of 'Britannia' class engines. Much of this was in studying the closely knit workings in East Anglia, but on the Western Region I went as far as Penzance and, on the Southern, to Dover. I also

On the Caledonian line: Manchester–Glasgow express crossing the River Clyde near Crawford hauled by 4–6–2 No. 70050 *Firth of Clyde* in 1961

Derek Cross

had the interesting experience of riding in the dynamometer car when one of these was on test between Rugby and Euston. These observations extended to 13 individual engines and 15 different crews. I can say at once that when still relatively new, and before the accumulated running mileage had begun to mount up, they were not very pleasant engines to ride. I can quite appreciate that to a novice the experience of riding any express steam locomotive at speeds of 70–80 mph could be something rather startling, in the stark contrast it provides to travel in the comfort of one of the passenger coaches; but I came to the 'Britannias' with many thousands of miles of footplate riding behind me, on routes extending from Penzance to Wick, from Ramsgate to Haverfordwest, and on a great variety of British locomotives large and small, good, bad and indifferent in quality of maintenance, and I did not find the 'Britannias' very satisfactory.

My first trip was from Liverpool Street to Norwich, on *Britannia* herself, when the engine was still quite new and before the schedules on that route had been accelerated. I was rather shocked at the hard riding and incessant vibration, though some of the latter originated in the method of coupling engine and tender used on the first batch of the new engines. In their policy of incorporating detail features that had proved successful on the regional types, the Railway Executive fitted the 'Britannias' with the very simple L N E R type of draw-gear between engine and tender consisting of one central bar; but while this was admirably suited to the smooth action of the Gresley three-cylinder 4–6–2s and 2–6–2s, it was not suited to the fore and aft oscillation of a two-cylinder engine, and with the 'Britannias' the result was horrible, not only on the footplate but often in the leading coaches of the train. It was replaced by the L M S type of draw-gear on later batches, having side buffers between engine and tender. Some of the engines allocated to the Western Region that I rode in 1951 were more comfortable in this respect, but the harsh clangour of their going was always prevalent.

Although so different from anything that they had previously been accustomed to, the Western Region men took the introduction of the 'Britannias' very seriously, and with their painstaking firing the steaming was much more consistent than on the same engines elsewhere. This was remarkable because three of the crews with whom I rode in the autumn of 1951 were on these engines for the first time. Both *Morning Star* and *Tornado* gave me some good running, though nothing that a 'Castle' could not readily have equalled. But on the incessant curvature of the line west of Newton Abbot I noted with pleasure that however much noise, dirt and vibration there was in the cab the engines gave an immaculate performance as *vehicles*, riding the curves smoothly and steadily, although the speeds in these conditions were generally less than 60 mph. My runs down in the West Country, added to the indifferent early experiences on the Great Eastern line, with somewhat erratic steaming, left me with rather mixed first impressions, which were confirmed when I came to the Southern. In mid-October 1951 engine No. 70004 *William Shakespeare* had only recently taken up regular work, after having been on exhibition at the Festival of Britain in London throughout the summer. 'She' was highly embellished and, as a prestige British locomotive, was put on to the Golden Arrow Pullman boat express between Victoria and Dover Marine, in each direction.

In arranging for me to ride the engine, however, my friends on Southern Region suggested that my footplating on the boat trains might be extended to give some variation in motive power, by making the round trip from the Dover end. The men who worked No. 70004 on the down Golden Arrow brought the inward-bound night ferry train from Dover, and as this was a heavy train usually worked by one of the 'Merchant Navy' class the contrast should be interesting, particularly with the same driver and fireman. So I went down on the previous evening on a 'West Country' 4–6–2, on the 5 p.m. residential express from Cannon Street, alighting at Sandling Junction to spend the evening with some friends who then lived at Hythe. Before we left the station the signals were pulled off for an up express, a boat train as it turned out, on which one of the new engines, No. 70014 *Iron Duke*, going great guns, made an impressive sight. There is no need for me to dwell upon the contrasts that were presented on the following day's round trip, except to say that while the Bulleid engine steamed with freedom the 'Britannia' did not.

We had no more than a moderate load of nine Pullmans and two vans, 395 tons behind the tender, but from the very start the engine was making heavy weather of it. All the way up to Knockholt summit we rarely had more than 180 lb per sq. in. in the boiler, and the driver was using

A one-time Eastern Region 'star', No. 70007 *Coeur de Lion*, after dieselization transferred to Scotland and here seen leaving Elvanfoot in Upper Clydesdale on the early morning stopping train from Carlisle to Glasgow in 1964   *Derek Cross*

between 30 and 40 per cent cut-off with full regulator most of the way. The easy run downhill to Tonbridge enabled things to be rallied, but it was not until we had observed a temporary speed restriction east of Paddock Wood that the running became more truly representative of what those engines could do. Then from Staplehurst on the gradual rise to the summit point at Westenhanger, on an average gradient of 1 in 680, we averaged 67.3 mph for 22.3 miles. But in giving due praise to this effort I could not help recalling that before the war, on the outward-bound night ferry train with a considerably heavier load of 440 tons, a 'Lord Nelson' class 4–6–0, the *Howard of Effingham*, had averaged 68.2 mph over this same stretch. And this was in 1937, before the Bulleid modifications had so improved the capacity of those engines. The respective power outputs of the two engines, allowing for the gradient, were 1250 draw-bar horsepower by *William Shakespeare* and 1415 by *Howard of Effingham*.

It was only a week after my own trip on No. 70004 that the accident occurred with that engine, leading to the withdrawal from traffic of the entire 25 engines of the 'Britannia' class. Some disquieting incidents of the coupled wheels shifting on their axles had already been reported and corrected, one with the engine I saw going so well at Sandling Junction, the *Iron Duke*; but the mishap with No. 70004 *William Shakespeare* was far more serious and crystallized the underlying trouble which had led to previous incidents. Incipient slipping at full speed while on the inward-bound Golden Arrow boat train near Staplehurst, Kent, led to the breaking of a coupling rod, and it was very fortunate that the train was stopped without derailment. The driving wheel axles ran on roller bearings. In 1951 there was nothing novel in that, and prior to nationalization both the L M S and the L N E R had built and operated very successfully express passenger locomotives of maximum power so equipped. The 'Britannias', like the L M S 'Duchesses', had hollow axles, a practice that on the Great Western went back to the introduction of the 'Abbey' series

of four-cylinder 4–6–0s in 1922. I remember discussing this with Sir William Stanier when I was writing his biography. He told me that it was not primarily a question of reducing weight. At Swindon they were then starting to heat-treat the axles, which greatly improved the outside but did not at first penetrate to the centre. In boring out the axle the coolant affected the structure of the metal at the heart of the axle and gave an excellent uniformity throughout. The reduction in dead weight was a bonus.

In designing the 'Britannias' the B R folks rather overdid the boring out, and in pressing on the bearing housings, on certain engines there was barely enough metal in the axles to withstand the stresses set up by the pressing-on process and wheels came loose on the axles. It was evidently a borderline situation, because some engines that were subjected to very severe hammering under test conditions, both at Rugby and on the Settle and Carlisle line, showed no sign of this weakness, while even before the major incident with *William Shakespeare* there had been several cases reported. Though there was widespread concern in technical circles as the news of the temporary withdrawal of all engines of the class filtered through, it was very fortunate that nothing reached the popular press because otherwise the Staplehurst incident would have been blown up out of all proportion by those who take delight in denigrating anything new that takes place on the railways. The difficulty was solved by plugging the hollow axles for the length of the wheel fit, and no further trouble was experienced on that score.

In the summer of 1953 the Eastern Region arranged a diverse programme of footplate riding for me designed to give a fairly comprehensive view of the work that was being done in East Anglia. I rode six different engines on duties rang-

1965, and nameplates removed lest they should be stolen by souvenir hunters (!), engine No. 70035 formerly *Rudyard Kipling*, leaving Carlisle with the morning Crewe to Perth express   *Derek Cross*

116

117

ing from a heavy express goods to one of the two-hour London–Norwich 'flyers'. The last named, on the 3.30 p.m. down from Liverpool Street, was actually the first, and it was dangerously near being the only one. I do not think I have ever endured anything quite like the shattering racket of that fast run. These days one talks freely about 'jet lag', but that evening in Norwich I had 'foot-plate lag' with a vengeance. It was a thing I had never previously experienced. It was an extraordinary tensed-up feeling with a splitting headache that gave me a completely sleepless night, while I debated whether I could go through with the next day's programme, which was going to involve 363 miles of running, beginning with the 8 a.m. to Liverpool Street, via Cambridge. However, reflecting that the trains I was to ride were not timed so fast as that tearing 3.30 p.m. down, I made the effort; and I am glad I did, for it was an interesting and varied day. For the record the engine that played such havoc with my nerves was No. 70009 *Alfred the Great*.

On the next day I rode the gentle *William Wordsworth* up to London, on a train that did not involve any very fast running; then back to Norwich on *Rudyard Kipling*, but with 20 minutes extra in which to do the journey the run was a gentlemanly affair compared to the sound and fury of the previous afternoon. There were times, however, when this engine showed that it could be something of a termagant if driven harder. The third run of the day was back to London on the 7.20 p.m. express goods, a relatively light duty that the cockney humorist of a driver said was little better than having no train at all. With speed mostly below 50 mph between a number of stops there was no chance for the engine to get rough. It was No. 70010 *Owen Glendower*. The next day was a Saturday, when the Norwich expresses are not timed so fast and heavier loads are taken. My run

'Britannias' on the Western Region: engine No. 70028 *Royal Star* on the 3.55 p.m. London to South Wales express, passing Reading West Junction   *M. W. Earley*

120

down to Ipswich, on No. 70037 *Hereward the Wake*, with a twelve-coach train against the nine we took on the tearing 3.30 two days earlier, was perhaps the pleasantest of all. We had 85 minutes to cover the 69 miles to Ipswich, and finished exactly on time despite checks on the way down. No. 70037 was a quieter, more comfortable engine to ride, but like all the 'Britannias' I rode she steamed freely and did her work with good economy.

The surprise of the whole expedition in East Anglia was reserved for my return trip from Ipswich to London on that Saturday, with engine No. 70039 *Sir Christopher Wren* and again a heavy twelve-coach weekend load. Travelling down in the morning, with the same load, we had made a net time of 78 minutes from London, and leaving Ipswich seven minute late on the return I looked forward to an enterprising run. But adverse signals checked us badly at Manningtree and Colchester, and then just as we were getting nicely going again, past Kelvedon, the engine suddenly went into a violent slip. I thought instantly of *William Shakespeare* two years earlier, and wondered if we were going to have another broken coupling rod, because a slip at 72 mph is not at all desirable. And then, at intervals all the way up to London the engine had fits of slipping, sometimes even when steam was shut off! The inspector who was riding with me was very worried, making copious notes to report, and I learned afterwards that the engine was taken out of traffic and given a very thorough examination. But no explanation was found. It seemed like just another of the enigmas that surrounded those engines, and I was reminded of the schoolboy who suggested they should be known as the 'Conundrum' class, because they had been designed by a Mr Riddles!

Joking apart, however, the 'Britannias' did a good job in East Anglia. As I concluded an article

A 'Britannia' on the Midland line: engine No. 70030 *William Wordsworth* on a trial run with a fully-braked coal train near Harpenden   *E. D. Bruton*

I contributed to *The Engineer* in 1954, 'The impression gained from these journeys, covering a very fair cross-section of duties worked by the "Britannia" engines in East Anglia, is that the work put to them was generally well below their maximum capacity. At the same time the high steaming capacity of the boilers was used to make fast climbs of inclines such as Brentwood, and for short high speed efforts like the northbound start out of Ipswich. The engines are well liked by their crews, and appreciated by those responsible for motive power arrangements on the old Great Eastern Lines.'

Having said that, I am afraid that recorded fact does not permit me to make any such favourable generalizations about the performance of the engines that were rather sparsely distributed between the London Midland, Scottish and Western Regions. Between 1954 and 1960 I was travelling a great deal, and on ordinary journeys when I was a passenger I had only twelve runs behind them. Many of them showed very poor work and loss of time. Apart from occasional runs between Paddington and Bath, they included the West Coast main line between Glasgow and Preston, the Midland line between Manchester and St Pancras, working of the Cardiff engines northward to Hereford, and repercussions from poor work by the Holyhead engines on the Irish Mail. To get steam for a relatively good run up from Chippenham to Paddington on a cold morning, steam was shut off from heating apparatus for the carriages; and twice when I was waiting for the 4.15 p.m. from Paddington and it arrived seriously late, it appeared that there had been lengthy stops en route to raise steam. I cannot say that I ever had any journeys behind them that I could be enthusiastic over, and this is reflected in the relatively poor availability of the engines for duty. It is true they worked very long mileages between successive visits to Crewe for periodic repairs, but they took a long time to amass those mileages.

Many of the special features introduced on those engines proved troublesome in service. I am told that in one unguarded moment, privately, one of those most intimately connected with the design wished they had never heard of roller bearings. Quite apart from the initial troubles through the hollow bore of the axles having been made too large, it proved very difficult to deal with cracks on the wheel seats because of the difficulty in getting the bearings out. The self-cleaning screens in the smokeboxes did not last from one boiler washout day to the next, and on those engines allocated to the Western Region a device of Swindon design was substituted. The truth is, of course, that other than in East Anglia, where there was a definite need for them, the 'Britannias' were not really wanted and with the various niggling troubles that beset them they became unpopular with all who had to use them. After 1955 when the great modernization plan for British Railways was launched and attention became focused on the forthcoming introduction of diesel traction, the few 'Britannias' became nobody's babies. It was ironic that engines labelled as a British Standard should be so few in number at most of the sheds where they were based as to be regarded as non-standard.

Some of the few engines of the class that were stationed at Polmadie (Glasgow) were used from time to time on the double-home turns to Leeds via the G & S W and Midland route. Then they would be manned by Corkerhill (Glasgow) men in one direction and Leeds men in the other, and no one had any particular interest in them, in contrast to the care they were given in East Anglia. Other things being equal, one would have imagined that the fastenings of the slidebars would have been the subject of regular scrutiny. But the particular design, which E. S. Cox once described as elegant, was taken from Doncaster practice and had been used on the Gresley 'Pacifics', three-cylinder 'Moguls' and the 'Green Arrow' 2–6–2s; there were no records of any trouble from loose fastenings, but in applying this design to the 'Britannias' the forward end of the assembly was tucked close underneath the extended rear end of the valve chest, completely out of sight and almost inaccessible. On a common-user engine fastenings that are out of sight are not likely to get the attention they require, and sooner or later they work loose; but one would hardly imagine they would get to the state they had done on engine No. 70052 *Firth of Tay*, when it was working the night Midland route express from Glasgow to Leeds on 20 January 1960.

The bolts holding the bottom slide bars on the right-hand side rattled themselves out, the bars themselves fell clear, and nearing Settle in the early hours of a morning of wild wintry weather the cross-head and piston rod came completely loose, turned over and in so doing caught the rail of the northbound track and pulled it badly out of alignment. A freight train was approaching at that very minute, and on coming on to the distorted rail its engine lurched to the right, and tore into the sides of the carriages of the express train. There were many casualties. One is always shocked to hear news of any railway accident, particularly where loss of life is involved; but this one, occurring within sight of a place where I spent many happy boyhood years, depressed me more than most, not any less when we learned of the technical failure leading to the partial disintegration of the machinery of the locomotive. It was depressing in that it seemed to epitomize the disarray into which much of the steam locomotive stock of British Railways was then falling in face of the gathering onset of dieselization; but with the 'Britannia' engines there was a deeper cause of disillusionment. I wish I could be more enthusiastic about them, for while many of the older express engines of the old private companies were ending their days in a positive blaze of glory, the 'Britannias', not yet ten years old, most certainly were not.

There is of course no doubt that on their day they could do extremely fine work, and I had occasion to publish, in 1961, details of a run logged by a friend on which *Dornoch Firth*, checked for permanent way at the foot of the Beattock bank, maintained speeds between 38 and 44 mph for seven miles of 1 in 75 ascent, with a ten-coach train of 360 tons. This was a splendid piece of work, approximating in the power output involved to the maximum efforts made in the early trials at Rugby and on the Settle and Carlisle line. My own experiences with them, in 1960, were however all very poor, and not a credit to the last British express passenger locomotive class. One feels that the old saying, that 'the road to perdition is paved with good intentions', could well be applied to these locomotives; for in the idealism that determined to make them a blend of the best features of regional practice the knitting together, as in the case of hollow driving axles, self-cleaning screens in the smokebox, and the slide bar attachments, was not very happy. With four separate drawing offices involved I suppose it was really too much to expect complete success, despite the co-ordinating hand of E. S. Cox. Bond felt that a 'Mark 2 Britannia', incorporating all the lessons learned with the first lot, and *with three cylinders*, would have been a superb locomotive; but the edict of 1955 slammed the door on any such aspirations.

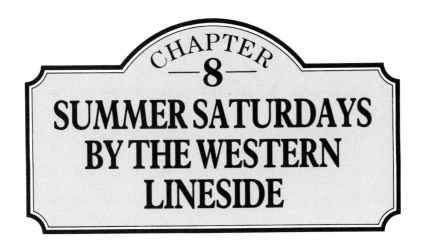

CHAPTER 8

SUMMER SATURDAYS BY THE WESTERN LINESIDE

After recalling the vicissitudes of the 'Britannias' it is a pleasure to turn to memories of many weekends of train watching and photography beside Western Region lines in the West of England on which my family and I were joined by friends from quite far afield, for what usually turned out to be a positive orgy of locomotive spotting. In the early and mid-1950s when petrol rationing was still in force, the holiday traffic to Devon and Cornwall on summer Saturdays was very heavy, and quite apart from mere number-taking, which the younger members of our parties pursued with great enthusiasm, the traffic operation provided so fascinating a study that we were more than once joined by professional railwaymen who came to some of our vantage points to see how things were going. Our holiday visits to Teignmouth and observations on that delightful sea-wall promenade had shown me that at many weekends the timetable would go completely haywire, with much late running; and so, before organizing full days out from Bath, designed to cover a maximum of trains, my friends at Paddington kindly furnished me with working time-tables which included the reporting numbers of all trains.

The preliminaries were as important as the need for fine weather on the day itself. Olivia, my wife, not only prepared mountains of sandwiches and other sustenance for the alfresco meals that would be snatched in brief intervals between successive trains, but she typed – with a copy for every participant, young and old – a complete list of the trains scheduled to pass. Their expected times were useful up to a point, but far more important were their reporting numbers, carried in huge white figures on the smokebox doors of all loco-motives. On summer Saturdays it was not only the 'specials' and extras that carried numerical identi-fication, and one looked out for '130' down, the Cornish Riviera Express itself, as much as for '438', the 8.07 a.m. Sheffield to Kingswear, or '240', the 8.50 a.m. Liverpool to Penzance. With those assiduously compiled lists we could pick them out, whether or not they came in the proper timetable sequence. The working timetable also gave the clue to locomotive allocations that might otherwise have been obscure, and much of the fun on those busy days arose from spotting very unex-pected engines on important express trains, as when Old Oak Common shed began to use the 5 ft 8 in. 2–8–0s of the '4700' class on trains like the Torbay Express.

Much preliminary reconnaissance was needed

before the sites for prolonged lineside observation were selected. We often had fifteen or more persons in all, men, women and children, and while the photographers had lineside photographic permits the others certainly did not, and sites had to be chosen where the cars could be parked and there was a good view of the trains without infringing upon railway property. One of the best bases of operation we ever had was the overbridge carrying a country lane across the railway just north of Whiteball summit. It was an excellent spot for the photographers; there was plenty of space to lay out a picnic, and the children could see everything to the best advantage. On our way down from Bath we used to go via Somerton and Langport, pausing for half-an-hour or so where the road crossed the main line about a mile west of Charlton Mackrell station. We got a few good photographs of up expresses there, but we were anxious to press on west of Taunton, where the flow of traffic on the direct London line was joined by all the complications from north of Bristol and South Wales. We paused occasionally at Beam Bridge, where the A38 road dives under the railway in the middle of the Wellington bank, but the geography thereabouts was not suitable for dallying and we passed on to the chosen spot north of Whiteball summit, just in Devonshire.

Turning over the copious notes of train working that I made at the time, in summer lineside expeditions in the years 1951–5, I am amazed at the intensity and complexity of the weekend train workings. Generally speaking 'King' class engines were reserved for the heaviest of the West of England trains, rarely made up to fewer than fifteen coaches. A few 'Castles' remained on their regular weekday workings such as the prestigious double-home turns between Newton Abbot and Shrewsbury, but for the most part they seemed to be used turn and turn about with the numerous 'Halls' that were taken from their weekday mixed traffic duties to help with the holiday expresses. In a single afternoon's observation at Teignmouth seventeen 'Halls' and sixteen 'Castles' were noted on express passenger trains, but none of the

'Britannias' stationed in the Western Region put in an appearance. Particularly on the trains from the north and South Wales the observations one could make west of Taunton were the outcome of the critical operations in the Bristol area, which had to be appreciated for the apparently indiscriminate engine allocation to be understood.

While the majority of the cross-country trains called at all major stations from Taunton westward this certainly did not apply at Bristol. Many of these trains catered purely for weekend holiday traffic and there would have been no point in taking them into Temple Meads station, occupying platform space and requiring station work once they were at rest. Such trains could have been run non-stop from Gloucester, Pontypool Road or Newport, for example, making their first calls to set down at Taunton, or even at Exeter. The former Great Western routes to Minehead and Ilfracombe were then still in operation, and there were enough trains from northern centres to both. Trains having no need to stop in Bristol were run by the avoiding line, taking the left-hand fork at Dr Day's Bridge Junction, and then turning on to the avoiding loop at North Somerset Junction. None of these trains was literally non-stop through the Bristol area. The service provided on summer Saturdays was immeasurably greater than the ordinary midweek timetable, and the men working the holiday trains, from sheds like Coleham (Shrewsbury), Tyseley (Birmingham), Cardiff and Ebbw Junction would not have known the road beyond Bristol. The train they were working had to be remanned, and they stopped on the Bristol avoiding line abreast of St Philip's Marsh sheds, where the present HST servicing depot is located. Some of the trains changed engines as well.

It could well be wondered what happened when the dense procession of trains from northern points of origin converged with those from London, at Cogload Junction five miles before getting to Taunton. At one time there used to be an awful jam in the approach to Taunton. There were only two lines through the station, and with many of the

Up Saturday relief Cornish express approaching Whiteball summit, hauled by double-chimneyed 4–6–0 No. 6010 *King Charles I*   *K. H. Leech*

north trains requiring to stop, and often running very late, the longer-distance non-stop runs of the London trains were frequently delayed. There was, however, a pair of goods lines round the back of the passenger station, and on Saturdays these were kept clear so that non-stopping passenger trains could use them and get ahead of a train standing in the station. But it was a slow business, because the junction points had to be negotiated very slowly and the curves on the goods lines were sharp. I remember being taken that way once in 1925 when I was travelling on the 3.30 p.m. from Paddington, hopefully non-stop to Exeter in three hours for the 173¾ miles, but with the Taunton and other delays we arrived 28 minutes late. In the 1930s, as part of the works undertaken for the relief of unemployment, Taunton station was completely rebuilt, and the four tracks through the new station were extended to Cogload Junction and westward to Norton Fitzwarren, where the branches to Barnstaple and Minehead diverged. Delays at Taunton thereafter became much reduced.

Even on summer Saturdays the Cornish Riviera Express had preferential treatment, and the timetable gap in front of it was greater than for many other trains to allow for some recovery in case of late running. Its first stop was at Newton Abbot, not for passengers but to take an assistant engine over the severe gradients of the South Devon line, and by the time it had passed Exeter the *scheduled* timetable clearances in front of it had narrowed considerably. It would not have needed much late running to cause severe bunching of such a procession as shown in Table 4. On a day in 1954 when I travelled down from London on the engine of the Cornish Riviera Express we passed Exeter practically on time and it was only at Dawlish Warren that we began to get signal checks, but even so we were only six minutes late on arrival at Newton Abbot. The long procession of trains ahead of us

Table 4

Scheduled arrival time at Newton Abbot (p.m.)	Train
12.28	7.30 a.m. Birmingham to Paignton
12.45	6.35 a.m. Walsall to Kingswear
12.56	6.55 a.m. Wolverhampton to Paignton
1.10	8.50 a.m. Paddington to Paignton
1.16	9.30 a.m. Paddington to Newquay
1.26	7.30 a.m. Paddington to Kingswear (via Bristol)
1.31	9.40 a.m. Paddington to Paignton
1.43	6.40 a.m. Leicester to Paignton
1.55 (pass)	10.20 a.m. Paddington to Paignton
2.00	Cornish Riviera Express (1st part)

must all have been running very near to schedule time.

At Exeter the operating situation was more complicated than at either Taunton or Newton Abbot, because of the intersection of a major Southern Region route leading to the north coast holiday resorts and the former London and South Western route to Plymouth via Okehampton and Tavistock. The westward flow came from Brighton and Portsmouth as well as from Waterloo, and although its density was not to be compared with that on the Western Region lines the most careful timetable planning was necessary, not only because of the junction layouts immediately at the western end of St David's station, and at Cowley Bridge, 1¼ miles on the Bristol side, but because the flow of traffic was in a contrary direction to that of the Western Region trains. Thus, the westbound Atlantic Coast Express came down the hill from Exeter Central, intersected the down Western Region tracks and, after stopping in St David's station, made off in the direction of Bristol before turning left at Cowley Bridge Junction. On Saturdays the Atlantic Coast Express ran in

12.05 p.m. Saturday – Paddington–Penzance express descending the bank between Bruton and Castle Cary, and hauled by 5 ft 8 in. 2–8–0 of '4700' class

K. H. Leech

several sections, and these were scheduled to pass through St David's at times when the station was very busy with Western Region trains. Fortunately there were three running lines for each direction of traffic, so that it was possible for a Western and a Southern train to be standing, doing platform work, while a non-stopping train had a clear run through. It was the intersection routes that were likely to cause delay in the event of late running.

A tally of the up (Western) and down (Southern) traffic passing through the station in the two hours from 1 p.m., as shown in Table 5, will give some idea of the intensity of the working. The analysis

Table 5

Time (p.m.)	Train
1.06	Paignton–Bristol arrive
1.11	Penzance–Paddington arrive
1.12	Paignton–Bristol depart
1.15	Down Southern arrive
1.20	9.20 a.m. St Ives–Paddington passes
1.22	Down Southern depart
1.26	Penzance–Paddington depart
1.27	Down Southern arrive
1.31	Down Southern depart
1.36	Newquay–Paddington passes
1.50	Paignton–Manchester arrive
1.50	Down Southern arrive
1.54	Down Southern depart
1.58	Up Cornish Riviera passes
2.00	Paignton–Manchester depart
2.05	Down Southern arrive
2.09	Down Southern depart
2.13	Kingswear–Birmingham arrive
2.18	Paignton–Paddington passes
2.22	Kingswear–Birmingham depart
2.28	Penzance–Liverpool passes
2.35	Paignton–Paddington passes
2.40	Down Southern arrive
2.42	Newquay–York arrive
2.45	Down Southern depart
2.48	Paignton–Wolverhampton passes
2.50	Down Southern arrive
2.51	Newquay–York depart
2.52	Down Southern depart
2.53	Penzance–Cardiff arrive
3.00	Newquay–Wolverhampton passes
3.04	Penzance–Cardiff depart

of that rather amazing procession shows six Western trains and six Southern stopping at Exeter, and seven going through non-stop; 19 express passenger trains in two hours, with an average headway of $6\frac{1}{4}$ minutes, between Exeter and Cowley Bridge Junction.

In studying these times it will be appreciated why some of the Western Region trains had what appeared to be unduly long station stops at Exeter. The Penzance–Paddington arrival at 1.11 p.m. was a case in point. It was one of the trains making many intermediate stops, and had to wait to give preference to one of the Southern trains and to the passage of the 9.20 a.m. from St Ives to Paddington. This latter was one of the holiday trains making very long non-stop runs. It was actually an advance section of the Cornish Riviera Express, and had no passenger stop east of Truro. To avoid congestion at Plymouth it stopped to change engines at Laira Junction adjacent to the big motive power depot, and because the load was always far greater than the 360-ton maximum permitted to the 'King' class engines over the South Devon line it had to be double-headed as far as Newton Abbot. The actual non-stop run was therefore from the point of setting down the pilot engine, just short of Newton Abbot station. Another long run among those passing Exeter in those hectic two hours from 1 o'clock was that of the 2.28 train, which would have been running nominally non-stop from Plymouth to Pontypool Road. I do not recall what the locomotive working arrangements were for this train, but they would no doubt have involved remanning at St Philip's Marsh, Bristol.

On one busy Saturday I spent some time with the locomotive control staff at Newton Abbot, and was very interested to find how differently they had to view the constantly changing situation from an outsider like myself, watching from the lineside or from the station platforms. In talking to those dedicated operators I was reminded of the celebrated wartime poster, 'There isn't even half an engine to spare.' Everything that could turn a wheel was pressed into service on those Saturdays, and I was interested to find the controllers more interested in the down trains than in the intense procession going north and east. As it was explained to me, the up trains I saw all had their engines. The down trains, many of them terminating at Paignton, had engines on which they were relying for eastbound trains later in the day, and some of the turn-round times were pretty sharp. There were no turntables at Torquay or Paignton, and engines for up trains originating at Paignton had to be sent down from Newton Abbot tender first. One day when I was watching there were the makings of a serious delay because of this. Newton Abbot had one of their star engines, the 'Castle' No. 7000 *Viscount Portal*, earmarked for the 1.30 p.m. up non-stop from Paignton to Paddington, but prior to this it was booked to take the Torquay line portion of the 7 a.m. from Birmingham, due to arrive at Newton Abbot at 11.36. It was wired 34 minutes late, and No. 7000, running tender first,

did not get away with the Torquay line portion until 12.23 p.m. It was going to be a close thing, but all was well in the end and we saw the Paddington non-stop come through Newton Abbot on time.

Even though all sorts and conditions of engines had to be pressed into service on those hectic days, failures on the road were few and far between, at any rate when I was watching. But one afternoon when I was on the Teignmouth sea-wall the 1.50 p.m. from Kingswear to Paddington came past with a 'Castle' that shall remain anonymous, extremely dirty and looking in poor shape. Not long afterwards the 10.45 a.m. from Penzance to Sheffield came up, and was stopped by signal at the entrance to Parsons Tunnel; and there that train

10.05 a.m. Penzance–Liverpool express near Whiteball summit, hauled by 4–6–0 No. 6908 *Downham Hall*   *K. H. Leech*

sat for a solid half-hour. That very shabby 'Castle' had failed completely at Dawlish and a rescue operation had to be mounted from Exeter. The only other case I personally noted was on the 12.30 p.m. Paignton to Manchester when I was travelling passenger to Bristol. The engine was a 'Britannia', and soon after leaving Exeter it became evident that it was steaming poorly. Fortunately the loss of time had not become serious until we had left Taunton, so that it was only the north country and Welsh trains behind us that were delayed. This was just as well, because the most that engine could do on the level stretches north of Bridgwater was 45 mph. Even on the very busiest days when motive power of any kind was at a premium one saw hardly any 'Britannias'. The ex-Great Western engines had the field nearly all to themselves.

It is pleasant, if a little sad, to look back to those leisured days by the Western lineside; after having conveyed my friends and their apparatus my part in organizing things was almost finished, and I could sit and watch the trains come by. Whiteball was my favourite place though in the late afternoon when traffic had thinned a bit we used to pause at a convenient spot near Cogload Junction where most of the trains were going a good deal faster than up at the summit. Those were the swelling, burgeoning days of passenger travel *en masse* rising to a climax on what used to be the Great Western Railway. With paid holidays for all, popular motoring barely emerging from the restrictions of petrol rationing, and railwaymen from all parts of Great Britain on their new-found B R passes flocking to the West Country to see if its advertised delights were really true, the numerous weekend trains were full to capacity. I remember the station master up at Kyle of Lochalsh telling me that he and his wife were going to spend their summer holiday at Penzance. Now that no restriction was put upon distance they were going to go as far as they could. Necessarily there were restrictions as to trains, because at that time the principal expresses like the Cornish Riviera left Paddington with every seat

reserved. Such restrictions applied to many of the regular trains, but after the privations of wartime few minded queueing up for and scrumming into one of the many extras. Unfortunately those who travelled no more than occasionally, and exclusively at weekends, gained the impression that those were the only conditions of rail travel.

At the lineside, of course, all eyes went to the engines that passed, and the loads they were hauling, and it was always pleasant for me to see once again engines that had been my footplate 'mounts' come thundering up the Burlescombe bank in gallant style: *Stokesay Castle, Trentham Hall, King Edward III, Lysander, Usk Castle, Caradoc Grange* – I would inevitably fall to reminiscing of my experiences with them, on this or that train: of *Stedham Hall*, which had just passed, treating her holiday load on a former occasion to an arrival nine minutes *early* at Dawlish; or *Earl St Aldwyn* blasting a way up that deadly first bank out of Kingswear with the Torbay Express and then running like the greyhounds all 'Castles' were on the non-stop run from Exeter to Paddington. On our way down from Bath one day, when we paused briefly at the overbridge near Charlton Mackrell in time to see *King Henry V* come past with one of the earliest expresses from the West Country, I could not help remarking as we set out again, 'Once more into the breach, dear friends.' Two very youthful visitors in our party, not yet in their teens, had no such respect for old acquaintances in the locomotive world. They were intent, so it seemed, only on ticking off engines they saw in their ABC spotters' books, and when an engine came along that they had seen before they would scream 'Scrap it!' as the train passed. Alas, for many locomotives we saw on those lineside expeditions, that childish admonition was to come true all too soon.

Sentiment and juvenile reactions apart, however, in looking back over my old notes it is to appreciate once again what a massive job of transportation the Western Region and its locomotives were doing on those Saturdays, and the organization that lay behind it. The train-

numbering system, displayed on the locomotive smokeboxes, originated in 1934, but in the post-war years with a greatly augmented timetable most of the individual train numbers were changed. Of the three-figure numbers the first digit represented the operating division in which the train originated. Down in the West it was simple so far as up trains were concerned. The Exeter Division covered Newton Abbot and the Torquay line, and the numerous trains starting from Kingswear and Paignton all had numbers beginning with 5. The Plymouth Division trains,

Penzance to Paddington express taking water at the troughs near Cogload Junction, and hauled by 'Castle' class 4–6–0 No. 5060 *Earl of Berkeley*

K. H. Leech

Wolverhampton–Weymouth express near Castle Cary, hauled by one of the few surviving 'Star' class 4–6–0s No. 4061 *Glastonbury Abbey*   *K. H. Leech*

including everything from Cornwall, began with 6; so the up Cornish Riviera was 635, the 10.05 a.m. Penzance to Liverpool 660, and the 11.15 a.m. Newquay to Wolverhampton 678. In the down direction it was rather more complicated, because of the more diverse origins: 1 from London, 2 Shrewsbury, 4 Bristol, which of course included all the trains taken over from the London Midland Region, 7 from South Wales, and 8 from Birmingham and Wolverhampton. Nevertheless,

identification was not entirely free from hazards, which all added to the fun of the game. Sometimes, when engines were making a quick turn-round, the numbers on the smokebox were not changed. I often saw the 1.15 p.m. from Paddington to Weston-super-Mare with the engine carrying the figures '455', which related to the 9 a.m. up from Temple Meads on which the engine would have worked up to London. But on Saturdays, when there were so many extra trains, care was always taken to make sure they were accurately labelled.

I cannot end this chapter without a reference to one of the most interesting of the holiday workings, the Cornish Riviera Express west of Newton Abbot, and the immediately following 10.35 a.m. from Paddington. While in pre-war days the train was famous for the number of slip coaches it carried, and for the diversity of West Country destinations served thereby, on summer Saturdays in the 1950s the entire fourteen- or fifteen-coach train went through to St Erth, and that of the following 10.35 a.m. to Truro. Both needed double-heading from Newton Abbot, and an interesting proceeding was adopted. The Cornish Riviera itself had no passenger stop until Truro; so it was provided with *two* fresh engines from Newton Abbot and went on literally non-stop, being booked to cover the 85.5 miles in 138 minutes. In the meantime the engine that had worked the Cornish Riviera down from Paddington, having coupled off at Newton Abbot, was available to double-head the 10.35 to Plymouth. Although the 10.35 was always a heavy train, usually with nine of its fourteen coaches for Penzance and five for Falmouth, when I saw it the engine was most frequently a 'Castle'. The timing was a little easier on Saturdays, and I have seen it arrive at Newton Abbot slightly *ahead* of time, with a fourteen-coach train. On one occasion,

Paignton and Torquay to Manchester express on the Teignmouth sea wall, hauled by the pioneer G W R four-cylinder 4–6–0 No. 4000 *North Star*, rebuilt as a 'Castle'
E. D. Bruton

however, both the 10.30 and the 10.35 were hauled by 'Kings', and after the first named had left with two fresh 4–6–0s, the departure of the 10.35 was impressive indeed with *King Charles II* and *King Richard III* in double harness. That particular day was also notable because the 10.20 a.m. from Paddington, running just ahead of the Cornish Riviera all the way down from London and having a headway of only five minutes to clear on to the Torquay line at Newton Abbot, was worked by one of the 5 ft 8 in. 2–8–0s, No. 4706.

I was very interested in the working of the Cornish Riviera Express at the height of the holiday season, and the Western Region authorities gave me a footplate pass to see everything at first hand. Coming down from Paddington on *King William III* we had a wonderfully clear road as far as Dawlish, from where it was evident that the close procession of trains for the Torquay line were bunched up ahead of us, and with many signal checks in consequence we were six minutes late arriving at Newton Abbot. There, as usual, the 'King' coupled off and was replaced for the non-stop run to Truro by *Caradoc Grange* and *Wolseley Hall*. The gross train load was 500 tons, 465 tons tare, and the division of 233 tons each to our two fresh engines meant that they were not far short of the maximum of 288 tons allowed to engines of these classes over the very severe gradients of the South Devon line. There was another factor to be taken into account in assessing the merit of the performance. There are no water troughs anywhere west of Newton Abbot. The tenders of the 'Grange' class engines hold 3500 gallons of water and those of the 'Halls' 4000 gallons, and although the 'Grange' was the more powerful engine of the two, because of its smaller coupled wheels the driver could not afford to pound the engine unduly, having regard to his lesser supply of water.

Saturdays-only St Ives to Paddington express passing Wolfhall Junction, near Savernake, hauled by engine No. 6017 *King Edward IV*   *Ivo Peters*

The line, of course, is a steeply graded switchback throughout, with alternations between hammering away at 25–30 mph uphill, and running downhill practically without steam. It is the kind of road on which a great deal of water can be wasted by careless or inexpert firing. It is all very well to go storming up a heavy gradient with a full head of steam in the boiler; but on topping a summit the change in conditions is immediate, the regulator is closed and demand for steam ceases abruptly. Unless firing while on the bank has been carefully regulated there will be too much steam in the boiler, the safety valves will lift and much of it go to waste. I rode on the leading engine of the two, the *Carodoc Grange*, and the Plymouth men who handled her were a couple of real artists. On all the heavy gradients the pressure of steam in the boiler was allowed to fall a little as successive summits were neared, with the result that never once on the 85-mile non-stop run did the safety valves blow off. And there was always plenty of steam when the driver needed it for hard work. Remarkably, we also got an absolutely clear road through Plymouth, and just afterwards made a fascinating way past the dockyards of Devonport, and then at dead slow speed to the crossing of Brunel's masterpiece, the Royal Albert Bridge over the Tamar, and so into Cornwall.

Not far inshore from the left bank of the Lynher River one is in the presence of railway history, for it was here that Brunel took the single-tracked Cornwall Railway much nearer to the shore than the present line, and crossed the creeks with some of the most beautiful of his timber trestle viaducts. From St Germans it is hard pulling up to the high moors around Liskeard, but our two engines were doing famously, and when we passed Liskeard station, 49½ miles from Newton Abbot in 77 minutes, our initial lateness had been wiped out and we were a minute early. Nevertheless as we topped the summit and dipped down that

Up West of England express, on the sea wall beside the River Teign, approaching Teignmouth hauled by engine No. 6007 *King William III*   *E. D. Bruton*

gloriously wooded valley that leads to Lostwithiel I must say I looked anxiously at the water gauge on the tender. We had only 1,000 gallons left, and still more than 30 miles of switchback railway to go. There is a fearsome little 'peak' in the track after Lostwithiel, up to Treverrin Tunnel, and then down to tide-water at Par; up again, past the far-famed Carlyon Bay golf course, on the cliff edge, to St Austell. The serried array of gleaming white peaks on the right of the line, from the china clay workings, once prompted a fellow traveller to assure us that they could be seen from the Scilly Isles, though what you can actually see are the similar tips more than 40 miles west of St Austell – at St Just, near Land's End. Speed was little more than 25 mph at the Trenance viaduct on my footplate run, at the top of the stiff pull up from Par sands; but we were well on time now, and with a pleasant gallop over the final switchback we came in sight of the city of Truro and its beautiful cathedral in good time for an arrival several minutes early.

But on a summer Saturday it was too much to hope that our luck with clear signals would last to the end and sure enough we were stopped outside the station while an earlier train finished its platform work. Our actual time for the $85\frac{1}{2}$ miles from Newton Abbot was exactly the 138 minutes scheduled; but allowing for the final stop and two slowings for permanent way work en route, our net time was only 124 minutes, an average speed of 41 mph over this very difficult road. On arrival we had 500 gallons of water left in the tender of *Carodoc Grange*, and a check with the enginemen of the *Wolseley Hall* showed that they had used about 3000 gallons on the run, a comfortable margin on both engines. Of course there would have been times when things were not so favourable, and then the non-stop run would have had to be abandoned to enable one, or both, of the engines to have a fill-up at one of the intermediate stations. All in all, the Western men and their engines were doing a great job in those now long-past summers.

CHAPTER 9

THE GHOSTS OF CAMDEN

On the left, leaving Euston for the north and little more than a mile out of the terminus, there used to be a large engine shed. Not a trace of it remains today for the site has been cleared and the space covered with tracks whereon main-line coaching stock is stabled during the brief intervals between high-speed runs out on the line. The whole area hereabouts used to be a veritable hive of railway activity, extending back to the very beginning of the London and Birmingham Railway, when its first roundhouse – the building with the conical roof still surviving some distance to the right of the present main line – was established at the top of the Camden incline. I went to the main running shed one Sunday afternoon towards the end of the steam era to photograph the engines. Sunday seemed a good idea because then I hoped that there would be more of them than usual on shed. But as I wandered round photographing 'Jubilees', 'Converted Scots' and 'Duchesses' I found myself getting more wrapped up with the past, rather than with the present, impressive though the modern steam power was in its massed array there. I had been familiar with the shed, as seen from the passing trains, for upwards of forty years, and on that quiet Sunday afternoon it is perhaps not surprising that I sensed there were quite a few ghosts lingering in odd corners.

The title of this chapter was suggested by a magnificent painting by Terence Cuneo of an imaginary scene at nightfall on the tracks outside the modern Euston. The centrepiece of the picture, entitled 'Into the 80s', showed in breathtaking splendour one of the APT sets striding out into the night, but standing discreetly in rear at the head of adjoining platforms with steam up ready for the 'off' were some of the ghosts of 'Euston Past'. It delighted me, because it was an assurance that I was not the only one who was conscious of ghosts around that first mile out of Euston. Inevitably one of them was a 'Duchess' proudly carrying the nameboard *The Royal Scot*; but Cuneo's imagination and exquisite draughtsmanship carried the ghost story back much earlier. Not quite obscured by the emergent APT was a 'George the Fifth' class 4–4–0, admittedly decked in Midland red, while at the next platform to the 'Duchess' was a Webb four-cylinder compound 4–4–0 of the 'Jubilee' class. It was, I suppose, inevitable to find a Midland compound lurking in the background, and although one's gorge rises slightly at the thought of such an engine in so essentially a North Western stronghold, in all fairness one must agree that those alien engines did some good work on the Birmingham two-hour expresses in the early Grouping days. Though it has no more to do with steam than the APT, I was glad to see as another background personality the very first British main-line diesel electric locomotive, L M S No. 10000, of 1947, assuredly another of the 'ghosts'.

I had been a very puzzled spectator of the sad epoch after Grouping when the merging of Midland with London and North Western ideas was so clumsily and tactlessly pursued as to set everyone by the ears, reduce morale to its lowest level ever, and the actual running of the trains to a state of slackness and indifference unbelievable to those who knew the London and North Western Railway of old. The public image of the West Coast main line was not helped by one writer in particular in the popular railway press of the day, who seemed to have no grasp whatever of the essentials of the situation, which lay in personal relations rather than nuts and bolts. Deterioration in performance was represented as stemming from ageing of the

machinery due to intensive utilization in earlier days, whereas in fact many of the top-line passenger engines of the early and mid-1920s had been built new since the war. My sense of disbelief and the feeling of ignorance, if not necessarily unfairness or bias, in the then current presentation of affairs on the Euston route to the north, led me to much study and investigation; and I cannot say it was finished until I was invited to write a definitive history of the work of C. J. Bowen Cooke, which was published in 1977. In that book I hope I laid to rest for all eternity some of the ghosts of the L N W R locomotive practice, but in so doing I

Two 19th-century 'ghosts' in Euston: a 'Teutonic' class three-cylinder compound and a 2–4–0 'Precedent' class alongside   *British Railways*

142

revived memories of men and machines that I hope will never die. And those memories are inextricably linked up with the very last years of steam on the West Coast main line.

Camden shed, unlike its great and friendly rival in the adjoining parish in North London, had always been concerned almost entirely with mainline express passenger work. The freight engines were quartered at the much larger shed out at Willesden, where the London Division locomotive superintendent and his running inspectors were based; Watford looked after the tank engines on the commuter runs, while the longer-distance residential trains were powered by Bletchley engines. From Camden 'Pacifics' went out on 401-mile through workings to Glasgow, to be remanned at Carlisle, and men would rarely get the same engine when they returned next day. Not even the most senior top-link men had 'their own engine'; the principles of maximum utilization did not tally with the exigencies of the eight-hour day and union requirements where high mileages were concerned. A Camden engine, or I suppose I should say an engine starting from Euston, would go north on the Night Scot arriving in Glasgow about breakfast time, and be serviced ready to take the Midday Scot back to London at 1.30 p.m. The whole policy of modern locomotive design was governed by the need to make everything needing attention between trips readily accessible, and all the working parts robust and free from all incipient defects. Appreciating this kind of utilization, the ghosts of Camden past begin to loom up, and I shall always remember reading of the retirement of a famous driver in 1915, and of the engines that had been 'his'. This was David Button, who had been ace driver at the shed from 1891 until he retired.

In these days when individuals of considerably less dedication and accomplishment burst into print with reminiscences, or employ ghost writers to compile their life stories, one can only regard it as unfortunate that a man of Button's experience with locomotives did not communicate his memories to anyone. Probably he was far too

modest, but fortunately the *L & N W R Gazette* secured a few details of the engines he worked at the time of his retirement: the 'ghosts of Camden' indeed! During his twenty-four years of tip-top link running he drove only eight engines regularly. On each of them he was partnered by another top-link man, and those engines were driven by no one else. His partners were first Jesse Brown, and then Peter Jarvis. They worked only two trains, the 12.10 p.m. Liverpool and Manchester express from Euston to Crewe, and back with the 5.02 p.m. up, and then the famous 2 p.m. Scotch corridor train, and the corresponding southbound train at 7.32 p.m. from Crewe. Both involved a long day's work for engines and men, and while the engines were on the job continuously for months at a time the men worked every other day. Of course there would be times when the regular engines would be 'stopped' for minor repairs or for overhaul at Crewe; but some of those engines had a wonderful record of reliability, running from three to four months, six days a week, without any attention whatever other than routine day-by-day servicing.

What a pageant Dave Button's regular engines would have made if posed alongside for their photographs. His longest innings of all was on the Webb three-cylinder compound 2-2-2-0 *Jeanie Deans*, the only one of the ten 'Teutonic' class that was not named after a White Star liner, sailing from Liverpool, and the only one not stationed at Crewe North shed. Button and Jesse Brown, at Camden, had 'Jeanie', as they always called her, for eight years, from 1891 to 1899; but the stay of the four-cylinder compound 4-4-0s was relatively brief. Between 1899 and 1904 the two drivers had a 'Jubilee' No. 1911 *Centurion*, an 'Alfred the Great' class No. 1961 *Albemarle*, and then briefly, after Whale had altered the valve gear of the 'Alfreds', one of the modified compounds, the *Royal Oak*. Another star Camden engine at that time was the second of the 'Alfreds', No. 1942 *King Edward VII*, which alternated with *Albemarle* on the 12.10 and 2 p.m. departures from Euston. I shall always remember a story told to me by the

A Webb Jubilee class four-cylinder compound No. 1920 *Flying Fox* on a down express train consisting almost entirely of six-wheeled non-corridor coaches

C. Laundy

veteran photographer F. E. Mackay of the L N W R wanting a special 'official' photograph taken of the 2 p.m. Scotch corridor train, and of his horror at discovering that it was to be taken not at his chosen place, near to the site of the present Kenton station, or just south of Bushey, but at a locality to be selected by the Divisional Engineer at Stafford, emerging from Shugborough Tunnel.

Before he ever reached the site he was in dead trouble. As always he lived in Battersea, and made his way to Euston by the steam-operated Inner Circle line from South Kensington. The L N W R were not making things any easier for him because they issued a pass from Euston to Milford and Brocton, and to reach there he had to travel by a stopping train from Rugby. On that very morning the Inner Circle obliged with an engine failure, and for some time his train was stuck in one of the tunnels, and at Euston he missed the train that

would have connected with that 'stopper' from Rugby to Milford. However, finding that within half an hour there was an express non-stop to Stafford, the authorities, with great magnanimity, allowed him to travel on this, provided he paid the excess fare (fourpence) and walked back! Duly arrived at Milford and escorted to the chosen spot, he found it could not have been worse for train photography. The location itself is extremely picturesque but the view, from the outer side of a curve, meant there would be little seen of the train except for the engine and the leading coaches. One could not get farther away

In the breathtaking Lune Gorge: a
Glasgow to Morecambe express in July
1965 taking water at 75 mph from
Dillicar troughs: engine, 'Black Five' No.
44927
Derek Cross

The celebrated Stanier 'Pacific' engine
Princess Margaret Rose, maker of the
very fast run described in Chapter 9:
here seen at Perth
W. J. V. Anderson

The preserved 'Glen' class 4-4-0, member
of the very successful class that worked
the West Highland line for more than
twenty years: No. 256 *Glen Douglas* in
the colours of the North British Railway,
here seen at Auchtermuchty in May
1963
W. J. V. Anderson

OPPOSITE ABOVE: A famous one-time
habitué of Camden: the preserved 2-4-0
'Precedent' class record-breaker of 1895,
No. 790 *Hardwicke*, here seen at York.
On the last night of the race this engine
ran the Aberdeen express from Crewe to
Carlisle at an average speed of 67 mph.
J. C. Simpson

OPPOSITE BELOW: Still farther north: in
1962 one of the 'Duchess' class Pacific
engines No. 46247 *Duchess of
Devonshire* leaving Carstairs with the
morning Crewe-Perth express
Derek Cross

The beautiful Caledonian 4-2-2 No. 123 at Callander, on the Oban line, in November 1964
W. J. V. Anderson

The restored Highland 4-6-0 of the 'Jones Goods' type of 1894, on a regular service train at the picturesque terminus of the Dingwall and Skye line, Kyle of Lochalsh
W. J. V. Anderson

Two preserved Scottish celebrities double-heading an enthusiasts' special at Craigellachie, Banffshire in June 1962: the Great North of Scotland 4-4-0 *Gordon Highlander* leading, and the Highland 'Jones Goods' No. 103 next to the train
W. J. V. Anderson

Crossing the great Ribblehead Viaduct: the preserved Southern 4-6-0 No. 850 *Lord Nelson*, climbing with the Cumbrian Mountain Express
D. C. Williams

The preserved Midland compound 4-4-0 No. 1000 which as M R No. 2631 began her life in 1902 on the Settle and Carlisle line
D. C. Williams

OPPOSITE: Last stage of the southbound climb: *Flying Scotsman* crossing Aisgill Viaduct with the Cumbrian Mountain Pullman in July 1983
David Eatwell

Midland compound No. 1000, piloting the preserved 'Jubilee' class 4-6-0 *Leander* on the southbound Cumbrian Mountain Pullman on a snowy February day in 1983, climbing to Aisgill at Birkett Common
David Eatwell

Unusual and distinguished visitor: the restored 'KI' class ex-LNER 2-6-0 No. 2005 passing Helwith Bridge with the northbound Cumbrian Mountain Pullman, in March 1983
David Eatwell

The preserved 4-6-2 No. 46229 *Duchess of Hamilton* creating a magnificent spectacle climbing towards Helm Tunnel with the southbound Cumbrian Mountain Pullman in November 1983
D. C. Williams

from the line because at the foot of a shallow embankment was a small lake, and to get beyond that would have meant encroaching on private property.

Mackay did the best he could in the circumstances. At that time, because of the deficiencies of the Webb compounds, the traffic department had imposed the 'equal to 17' rule as the maximum for any train to be hauled by one engine. The minimum load of the 'Corridor' in 1903 was three twelve-wheeled diners, and seven ordinary corridor coaches, which would be equal to '16½', and on the day in question sure enough the train was double-headed. Mackay told me that the 2–4–0 'Precedent' class No. 862 *Balmoral* was kept specially burnished up to pilot the 'Corridor' and so she was on that day, coupled ahead of the *King Edward VII*. I asked if the L N W R folks were pleased with the special photograph and he replied, 'Oh yes, I suppose so, but I wasn't.' He had a way of breaking up the glass plate negatives of

any photographs that he did not like, and so *Balmoral* and *King Edward VII* on the down 'Corridor' passed into oblivion, together with all the other photographs he took on that ill-starred day.

In 1904 Button exchanged the *Royal Oak* for one of the first of the new 'Precursor' class 4–4–0s, No. 659 *Dreadnought*, built in June of that year; photographed at Euston in No. 6 platform at the head of the 2 p.m. 'Corridor', it became lionized in one of the famous 'F. Moore' coloured picture postcards. It was, however, while he was running his second Whale express passenger engine, the 'Experiment' class 4–6–0 No. 1987 *Glendower*, that Button had two experiences to which one would dearly have liked to hear his reactions. They were in 1909 and 1910 when a number of

The end of a famous L N W R locomotive which should have been preserved: the *Coronation* of 1911, first stages in scrapping, June 1940 *British Railways*

locomotive interchange trials with other railways were in progress, and on the two occasions when trains starting from Euston were involved Button, as the senior express driver at Camden shed, was chosen to act as pilotman to the visiting drivers. In 1909 he rode on the Great Northern large-boilered Ivatt 'Atlantic' No. 1449 on her trips between Euston and Crewe, and similarly in 1910 on the Great Western four-cylinder 4–6–0 *Polar Star*, both types then in their non-superheated condition. It would have been deeply interesting to know what such an experienced driver as Button thought of those two famous designs, because not long afterwards he was developing an almost fervent admiration for Mr Bowen Cooke's superheated L N W R express engines.

Two of the 'George the Fifth' class 4–4–0s came new to Camden shed at the end of 1910, No. 1294 *F. S. P. Wolferstan* and 228 *E. Nettleford*, the former being allocated to Button and his new partner, Peter Jarvis. As traditional at Camden shed, the two new engines alternated on the 12.10 and 2 p.m. departures from Euston, and many photographs were taken of both engines in action. When more 'Georges' were available, No. 1706 *Elkhound* was used when either of the two stars was stopped for one reason or another. That, however, was not very often in those halcyon days of the L N W R. After it was worked in, Button and Jarvis between them ran No. 1294 continuously for thirteen weeks, Euston to Crewe and back, 316 miles every weekday before even booking the slightest defect; and then the engine, far from showing any signs of high mileage or roughness, was doing so well that Button jocularly remarked one day that if he met Mr Bowen Cooke he was going to suggest that the name of the engine be changed to *Charley's Aunt*, which classic stage comedy was even then still running! What mileage those two star engines, 1294 and 228, finally amassed before going to Crewe for general overhaul is unfortunately not known today, but on the form they were showing in 1911 their yearly total could have been around 80,000 miles each.

In 1913, however, a new era was dawning on the L N W R. In July of that year Button was sent to Crewe to bring one of the new four-cylinder 4–6–0s of the 'Claughton' class down to Camden. It was No. 1191 *Sir Frank Ree*, named after the reigning general manager of the railway. As in the case of his earlier charges it was to be *his* engine, and he handled it from the moment of leaving the works, brand new, again with his junior partner Peter Jarvis. Together they continued working the same two trains. A second engine of the 'Claughton', No. 1161 *Sir Robert Turnbull*, was allocated to Camden shed at the same time, and the two big 4–6–0s took over the work previously done by the two 4–4–0s 1294 and 228. Button remained on top-link work with engine No. 1191 until his seventieth birthday, in June 1915, and by that time all the old conditions of working were changing. They were never to revert to the old order again. It is certainly true that when the first of the post-war 'Claughtons' was created as a very impressive mobile war memorial, named *Patriot* and numbered 1914, it was put on to the afternoon Anglo-Scottish express from Euston, and ran it daily from Euston to Crewe in the winter of 1919–20 for several months; but by then the locomotive workings were being completely changed, and for a time Camden shed had no such prestigious turns as the 12.10 and 2 p.m. of pre-war days.

The troubled early days of Grouping are best passed over without comment; but when from among the refuse of the in-fighting, technical bias and company propaganda the true L M S began to emerge, in the summer of 1927, Camden had an important part to play. From 1930 until the outbreak of war in 1939 I was a commuter between Watford Junction and Euston, and although I was often travelling considerably farther afield my almost daily journeys past Camden shed, morning and evening, gave me a comprehensive view of what was going on. Furthermore, friendship with some of the rising stars of Euston House gave me the background knowledge that was essential to a proper appreciation of what I saw out on the line. Throughout this period the 'Royal Scots', seventy strong, were the mainstay of the express passenger service. The 'Pacifics' came on the scene in relatively small numbers: two in 1933; another ten in 1935, plus the turbine; five blue streamliners in 1937, and ten more of the so-designated 'Princess Coronation' class in 1938, five streamlined in red and five non-streamlined. From the lineside, from discussion meetings at the Institution of Mechanical Engineers, and later from the footplate I witnessed the evolution of the 'Royal Scots' from a design conceived in little short of desperation, built in shipwreck haste and having many incipient faults, to one of the best express passenger 4–6–0s ever to run in this country. The story of that evolution could not strictly be considered part of the last years of steam but for the curious twist in sentiment concerning the later version of the design that developed.

One thing I shall always remember about the original type, the 'Royal Scots', which might be thought purely incidental but was actually most significant. The local train by which I usually travelled up to Euston passed Camden shed about 9.15 a.m., at which time the shed staff were putting the finishing touches on the engine for the 'Royal Scot' train. Winter and summer alike the engine worked through over the 299.2 miles to Carlisle. This was a tough assignment, not so much in respect to the tractive power involved, but to the coal consumption. The original 'Royal Scot' locomotives had the standard L M S six-wheeled tender as fitted to the three-cylinder compound 4–4–0s and to the 'Baby Scots', and while its modest water-carrying capacity of 3500 gallons was no handicap on a route so liberally equipped with water troughs as the former London and North Western main line, it carried no more than

A wartime Crewe-built express engine of 1916 with a name commemorating a tragic disaster at sea: No. 25673 *Lusitania* (originally L N W R No. 1100), and one of the last of the 'Prince of Wales' class 4–6–0s to be scrapped (not until 1949) *British Railways*

5½ tons of coal. On the run through to Carlisle, even if it is assumed that no more coal would be fired once Shap summit was topped there would be an average of 45 lb per mile available for the 270 miles from Euston. In favourable circumstances and at the speeds required in 1930 this would have left a reasonable margin, but in wintry weather, over a route particularly exposed to strong cross winds, it could be little enough, and I was not surprised, on reflection, to see the coal men at Camden stacking every lump of coal they could on to the tender of the engine for the 'Royal Scot' train. They used to pack extra large lumps along each side of the tender to form a support for a pile up to the maximum height that would pass beneath the loading gauge. There is at least one photograph of the 'Royal Scot' train, taken near Watford, in which the heap of coal is seen slightly topping the level of the cab roof!

Apart from that high stacking, which meant they were probably carrying at least one ton more than the rated maximum, and which was an outward and visible sign of their appetite for coal on these long runs, there was a more insidious and increasing disease that greatly worried the management of the L M S. The coal consumption of the 'Royal Scots' was rapidly rising as their mileage in traffic increased. At no shed was this increase more critical than at Camden, which with sixteen based at the shed had by far the largest allocation of the original fifty engines built in such haste in 1927. The changed circumstances from those of the greatest L N W R days are shown by a comparison of the 'Royal Scot' allocation to that of the 'Claughton' class 4–6–0s in 1917 (see Table 6). In L N W R days, while Crewe was very much the nerve centre of express passenger locomotive working – as evidenced by the massing there of no fewer than thirty-three out of the original sixty

---

Meeting the dawn on Shap: a steam-hauled relief to the 'Night Scot' in 1964, hauled by 4–6–2 No. 46225 *Duchess of Gloucester* half-way up the bank, near Scout Green   *Derek Cross*

Table 6

Shed	'Claughtons'	'Royal Scots'
Camden	9	16
Rugby	8	3
Crewe North	33	9
Edge Hill	5	9
Preston	2	—
Carlisle	3	7
Polmadie	—	6

'Claughtons' – Camden had been the shop window, as it were, providing the power for two of the most prestigious passenger duties. After the war, however, apart from the *Patriot* episode, all this changed for a while, and the 'Corridor' was run by Rugby engines and men, remanning and sometimes even changing engines at Rugby itself. But with the development of the Anglo-Scottish services in 1927 Camden men had to learn the road northwards, first to Carnforth and then through to Carlisle, and once the euphoria of the introduction of the 'Royal Scots' had passed, those London men, and the Carlisle men working home, had some anxious moments with their fifteen-coach trains when the weather was bad. Fortunately there were always pilot engines standing by at Oxenholme ready to give a hand when necessary. The modified type of piston valve fitted in the early 1930s cured the insidious weakness of steam leakage past the valves, and reduced coal consumption, but in the later 1930s the large Stanier-type high-sided tenders were fitted to the 'Scots', and these carried no fewer than nine tons of coal, thereby relieving the Camden and Carlisle drivers of any anxiety about coal on these long runs when the weather was bad.

The 'Pacifics' were anything but popular when they were first introduced, and among the friendly cherished ghosts of Camden-past must be ranged two spectres – the frustrating, even grim memories of the boilers first fitted to Stanier's giants *The Princess Royal* and *Princess Elizabeth*; for they were each what Scots enginemen would call 'a dreich steamer'. The trouble was made

many times worse because these engines were designed to work through over the 401 miles between Euston and Glasgow. A Carlisle fireman whom I knew well, and who was a real artist with the shovel on 'Royal Scots', put the case against the 'Pacifics' succinctly: 'The Glasgow boys come in and say "she won't steam", and you've 300 miles to go!' He might have added 'non-stop', and I saw for

myself on the footplate what a trial that long run could be with an engine that was shy for steam most of the way. The shaky reputation of these two original 'Pacifics' persisted long after their first introduction. I was at Euston House one afternoon in 1935, and with one of my railway friends walked over to see the up 'Royal Scot' train come in, which it did a few minutes early. The driver was one of the most experienced Camden men and his 'Royal Scot' engine was polished fit for the Royal Train. My friend spoke to him, saying that soon they

Another of Camden's ghosts: the Royal Train of Queen Victoria's day, hauled by three-cylinder compound engine No. 410 *City of Liverpool* of the 'Dreadnought' class   *British Railways*

151

would be having the new big engines, referring to the 1935 batch of 'Pacifics'. The driver pulled a wry face, and said, ' . . . if they're any good.'

It had been unfortunate that the first two 'Pacifics' had been introduced just as the 'Royal Scots' were touching absolutely top form, which made the men all the more ready to make unfavourable comparisons. The design staff had learned their lessons with the two original engines, and the ten built in 1935 were superb machines. This is not to say that those responsible for publicity on the L M S were not a little touchy over references to these engines. By that time I was in their confidence, and they impressed me with the importance of avoiding use of the class title 'Pacific' in referring to the new engines, because otherwise they might be confused in the popular mind with the Gresley 'Pacifics' of the L N E R. I was asked, always, to refer to them as 4–6–2s. Whether other people who wrote about locomotives were asked to do the same I do not know, but if so the exhortation must have fallen on deaf ears because in the railway press generally they were referred to as 'Pacifics'. As was their wont, the men were not long in finding a homely and affectionate nickname for the big engines they soon grew to appreciate from 1935; they called them the 'Lizzies'.

One could continue gossiping for entire folios over memories of a place like Camden, but I am now going to skip the years by very nearly a quarter-century to the summer of 1959, when I met for the last time in really active service the first of the new 'Pacifics' of 1935, No. 46203 *Princess Margaret Rose*, not yet a ghost twenty-four years on, as I shall explain later in this chapter. In July of 1959, when many diesels were working on the principal expresses from Euston to

Two generations of Camden express locomotives: in front, 4–6–0 No. 5826, of the London and North Western 'Prince of Wales' class, dating from 1911 and, behind, a 'Royal Scot' 4–6–0 of 1927

British Railways

the north, I had been at Crewe on signalling business, and the quickest way home to Bath was via London. The evening express from Liverpool to Euston, which in pre-war days had the fastest start-to-stop schedule on the L M S, was by then known as 'The Red Rose', and I was on the platform little more than minutes before it came in from Liverpool, headed not by a diesel but by a 'Lizzie', none other than No. 46203 *Princess Margaret Rose*. She looked grubby, as if not having seen a cleaner's rag for weeks. I piled into the crowded train and clocked the time of the start as I made my way along the corridors in search of a seat. As I got towards the front of the train the steady uniform roar of the exhaust was reassuring, and I was soon recording one of the finest runs I have ever noted south of Crewe.

Having climbed the bank to Whitmore we dashed down the gentle gradients through the Izaak Walton country. This descent is no Shap or Beattock, in fact after Standon Bridge the gradient eases out until it is little steeper than level track, and yet here the Royal Lady was whirling her great, crowded, 500-ton train along at 83 mph. An easing round the curve beyond Stafford, and then flat-out across the Trent Valley, with another maximum of 80 mph near Tamworth. Rugby, $75\frac{1}{2}$ miles, was passed in $74\frac{3}{4}$ minutes; already 11 minutes of a late start recovered, and harder still onwards until adverse signals checked us down to 15 mph at Bletchley. But nothing seemed to discourage the two stalwarts on the footplate, and they tore into it again, such that in the deep chalk cutting leading to the crest of the Chilterns at Tring, doing a steady 67 mph on the gradient, the engine was developing nearly 2000 horsepower. The final dash downhill towards London was, however, punctuated by an incident I would like to think was not symptomatic of the age in which we now live. We had reached 80 mph again and were still accelerating, when at Bourne End Junction, midway between Berkhamsted and Hemel Hempstead, we were stopped for the signalman to warn our driver and firemen to keep a sharp lookout ahead because he believed children had been placing stones on the rails. It proved a false alarm, but the delay was serious and had cost us nine precious minutes in running.

Nevertheless it did not take long for our driver to accelerate the *Princess* back to something of her former stride and for 15 miles the speed lay entirely between 70 and 79 mph. It proved to be the very last time I travelled into Euston on a steam-hauled train, and what a conclusion it was. Because of the delays experienced we were not able to make a better overall time than $159\frac{3}{4}$ minutes for the 158 miles from Crewe; but allowing for Bourne End and three other checks of lesser severity our net time was no more than 144 minutes, a noble effort indeed.

The *Princess Margaret Rose*, all 159 tons of her, is hardly a ghost, though her truly active days ended in 1963. Then, when she would otherwise have been scrapped, she was purchased by Butlin's and placed on static display in the holiday camp at Pennychain, near Pwllheli. There she remained, splendidly restored to her original L M S livery, until May 1975 when she was conveyed to Derby for overhaul prior to going to her present resting place at the Midland Railway Centre, at Butterley, near Ripley, Derbyshire.

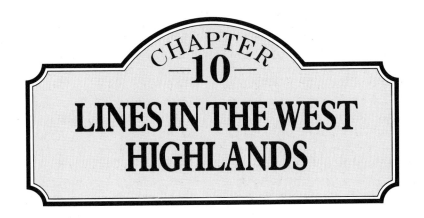

CHAPTER
—10—
LINES IN THE WEST HIGHLANDS

There is surely no railway that has become more romanticized than the West Highland itself and the extension to Mallaig opened in 1901. The variety and magnificence of the mountain scenery, the wildness of the weather sometimes encountered, and the associations with some of the most poignant and tragic episodes in Scottish Highland history all combine to create an atmosphere that anyone not completely absorbed by the mere nuts and bolts of a railway and its working cannot fail to find compelling. I travelled over it first in 1932, and was so overcome with a satiety of vivid emotions that I went again in 1934, 1936 and 1937. I stayed at various places on the line for weeks at a time and wrote long articles about my impressions. I was in Glasgow again in 1938, at the time of the Munich crisis, and on a Sunday between appointments I took the excursion to Mallaig. But the portents for Britain's future were so fearful that for once the line and the glorious country through which it fights its way to the north-west failed to work its magic. Although I have some Highland blood in my veins I have not 'the sight', and was not to know then that by the next time I came to travel to Mallaig the Nazi evil would have been overthrown and I should see detachments of prisoners-of-war working at the linesides. It would have been comforting though scarcely believable in 1938.

Turning to more prosaic matters, the locomotive problem on the line remained in 1946. The section between Craigendoran and Fort William – the West Highland proper – was built in 1894. The line was surveyed so that the track wriggled its way amid the rocky, mountainous terrain in such a way as to require the minimum of earthworks. The gradient that governed the maximum load that could be taken by the various classes of locomotives in use, the 'ruling gradient', was 1 in 55, though there were some short lengths on the Mallaig Extension line as steep as 1 in 45. But an additional handicap was the almost continuous curvature on some of the longest and most trying of the steep ascents, which, by reason of the sharpness of the radii, greatly increased the tractive resistance of the coaches or of the freight rolling stock. It goes almost without saying that a line in such rugged and mountainous regions was often subject to extremes of weather, though with the strict limitation placed on maximum speeds throughout the line strong winds were not such a hindrance as on a fast express route. From its junction with the riverside line from Glasgow to Helensburgh, at Craigendoran, there was officially a speed limit of 40 mph throughout; but it was not until I began my footplate work in 1937 that I became aware of this, and then in circumstances that could have been embarrassing.

During my earliest trips over the line in 1932 and 1934, when travelling passenger, I logged several instances of maximum speeds of 60 mph and slightly over, always on relatively straight stretches of line, such as the section across Rannoch Moor and on the downhill run towards Bridge of Orchy going south. The coaches always rode very smoothly, and I had no idea of the transgressions in progress. The speeds were included in some running details I sent to Cecil J. Allen for his use in *The Railway Magazine*, and they were duly published with no subsequent reactions other than appreciative comments from fellow readers, and from the Press Office of the L N E R at King's Cross, who were pleased to have some publicity for a route not hitherto in the news for its locomotive running. The largest engines then used on the line were the Class 'K2' 2–6–0s of Great Northern design, and because of the heavy gradients the maximum load they could take unassisted was 220 tons. In the summer tourist season many trains required to be double-headed, a practice that Sir Nigel Gresley abhorred. He had, a few years earlier, solved a similar problem on the East Coast main line between Edinburgh and Aberdeen by the introduction of the huge 2–8–2 express engines of the 'P2' class, which, as related in an earlier chapter of this book, were ruined by his successor. When it came to the West Highland line however he found himself rather inhibited by the physical conditions.

By use of the three-cylinder system of propulsion, however, lighter working parts, and coupled wheels reduced from 5 ft 8 in. to 5 ft 2 in., he was able to produce a locomotive that would take a 300-ton load without assistance. The civil engineer, while accepting a slightly higher maximum axle-load than on the 'K2', made the stipulation that the 'K4' class, as the new design was called, should on no occasion be double-headed. One engine only was built at first for trial purposes, the *Loch Long*, and in the autumn of 1937 I was favoured with an engine pass to ride her from Glasgow up to Fort William. Before the days of nationalization the L N E R did not put on an inspector when an outsider was given permission to ride on the footplate, and I had a pleasant and successful run with a very friendly Fort William driver and fireman. My return train was very heavy, and was double-headed by a pair of 'Glen' class 4–4–0s. True to reputation they put up an excellent show, but without an inspector at my elbow I was unaware they were considerably exceeding that 40 mph speed limit on certain sections, though the leading engine on which I rode was at all times steadiness itself in her riding. I wrote several articles, in a most enthusiastic vein, and as always when I had the privilege of an engine pass submitted the drafts for approval. They came back with every reference to speeds above 40 mph heavily struck out! I had some difficulty in presenting the logs of these runs in such a way that the instances where the limit had been exceeded were not readily apparent. In due course the articles were published, and all was well.

When I went back to the West Highland in 1946 the pioneer 'K4', the *Loch Long*, had been joined by five more engines of the same class, and they were doing excellent work. They were named after famous Highland chieftains, though at first those responsible for specifying the names got somewhat muddled up and the presentation incurred the wrath of some who were intimately connected with the clans concerned. When news of the trouble reached King's Cross it was whispered that the otherwise greatly revered Chairman of the company, Mr William Whitelaw, had been involved in the naming. Anyway, engine No. 3442, the first of the five, arrived at Fort William named *Mac Calein Mor* and the hackles of the local clans rose instantly. What did those Sassenachs in Glasgow think they were doing sending us an engine named after the arch enemy of old, the chief of the Clan Campbell! The engine was returned south in double quick time, and was taken into Cowlairs Works (it had actually been built at Darlington). In due course it returned north named *The Great Marquess*, and rumour once again had it that those who named the engine thought that the first and second titles referred to the same chap!

There was certainly no quarrel with the next two, *Cameron of Lochiel* and *Lord of the Isles*, and having by that time established a substantial majority, no one in Fort William minded very much when engine No. 3445 arrived with a slightly anglicized version of the Campbell chieftain's title *Mac Cailin Mor*. But all hell was let loose again when the last one arrived, for the name *Lord of Dunvegan* meant nothing. The Clan MacLeod rose as vehemently as Camerons and MacDonalds had done earlier, and engine No. 3446 soon had its name changed to *MacLeod of MacLeod*. The first engine of the 'K4' class, the *Loch Long*, was originally turned out in black, like the other West Highland engines of that time, but the 'chieftains' introduced in 1938–9 were regarded as something special and were painted in the pleasing apple-green livery of L N E R passenger engines. When I went up there after the war, however, to make a particular study of their working, they were all in plain black.

It was the first time I had travelled on the West Highland line in other than the summer tourist season, and with all my runs to be made on the footplate it was a tough experience, especially leaving Glasgow on the 5.50 a.m. before dawn on a March morning of sharp frost. My friend E. D.

Mallaig to Glasgow express leaving the Glenfinnan viaduct, hauled by 'K2' class 2–6–0 No. 4692 *Loch Eil*　　　　　　　　　　　　　　　*O. S. Nock*

Class 'K4' three-cylinder 2–6–0 No. 3446 *Macleod of Macleod*

British Railways

Trask was then Locomotive Running Superintendent of the Scottish Area of the L N E R, and with an interest and solicitude for my well-being he alone among those who then granted me engine passes always sent an inspector as my guide and philosopher. The regulations then differed from those of the L M S, in allowing two persons in addition to the driver and fireman on an engine. In the chill atmosphere of Queen Street station, Glasgow, a cheery little inspector named Graham made himself known to me, but just as we were about to climb up on the *Cameron of Lochiel* a tall young man, also clad in overalls, came up and he too presented a footplate pass. He was a pupil at Doncaster Plant, and his authority was an 'open' one for the West Highland line, without reference to any particular train. Inspector Graham explained the situation to him, and rather crestfallen he went away to find a seat in the train.

It was the first time I had met Graham, and with

his brief to look after me he was naturally watching points for the first half-hour or so of our journey, but when we were well under way and he saw I was no novice to footplate conditions, he told me he was going back to the train to tell the young man to come forward and take his place. He joined us on the *Cameron of Lochiel* at Arrochar and rode on the footplate for the rest of the way to Fort William, an enthusiastic and knowledgeable companion. It was not until 33 years later that I discovered his name, Peter N. Townend, when we were both guests of the North Yorkshire Moors Railway, as briefly mentioned in my previous book *On Steam*. In much later years he was shedmaster at King's Cross and wrote an entertaining and finely illustrated book about it, *Top Shed*. From the viewpoint of engine performance the run that morning was not one of my best. The engine was not steaming freely and we made heavy weather of the steep gradients, but later experience confirmed my earlier impression that neither driver nor fireman was particularly expert. They were a cheery enough couple, and the fireman worked like a Trojan, but it looked to me like the efforts of a country yokel rather than a practised engineman.

The circumstances were extenuating up to a point. During the war the older arrangements for manning on the West Highland line had changed, and crews no longer worked through between Glasgow and Fort William on lodging turns. This early morning train was booked to cross the

Fort William to Mallaig train, with the majestic crags of Ben Nevis in the background, as the train approaches Corpach. The engine is 'K4' class 2–6–0 No. 61995 *Cameron of Lochiel*   *E. D. Bruton*

9.31 a.m. express from Fort William at Spean Bridge, but if the 5.50 a.m. down was running late, as it sometimes was in those difficult years, the 'cross' and exchange of enginemen took place at Tulloch. It was a very strenuous round for the Glasgow men, because they were on the road continuously from 5.50 a.m. until 2.05 p.m. – that is if they got back punctually. After the introduction of the 'K4' engines in 1938–9 some diagrams involving intense utilization were put into operation and, with the wartime rearrangements for manning, an engine would regularly be handled by four different crews in working from Glasgow to Fort William and back. The Eastfield (Glasgow) men were at something of a disadvantage in the diversity of routes and engines that they worked, whereas the Fort William men were specialists, *par excellence*, in the running of this very severe mountain road. With a Fort William man on the shovel, engines that would not steam were unheard of.

I shall always remember a wet spring afternoon

Preserved Scottish locomotives in partnership, leaving Oban: the Caledonian 4–2–2 No. 123 and the North British *Glen Douglas*   *G. W. Morrison*

when with an engine pass in my pocket I was at Crianlarich waiting for the late train to Fort William. The skies were lowering, rain-sodden clouds were drifting over the mountains all around us, and there were few people about. No more than a couple of minutes behind time the train arrived from the south behind a very dirty and travel-stained 'K4', the *Lord of the Isles*, looking the very antithesis of the proud name it bore, but on the footplate were a pair of absolutely super Fort

Another distinguished pair: the G N S R *Gordon Highlander* and the beautiful 'Jones Goods' of the Highland, in the original yellow livery hauling an excursion train in Glen Fiddich between Craigellachie and Dufftown on the G N S R line
W. J. V. Anderson

William enginemen. They were old friends of mine, but the greeting they nodded to me was at first no more than perfunctory. They had taken a southbound train as far as Ardlui, at the head of Loch Lomond, crossed the train from Glasgow there and taken over its engine, with the news that it wouldn't steam. And the first thing they had to do was to drag that heavy train up one of the longest and most trying of all the gradients of the West Highland, Glen Falloch! They were not amused, and the moment they stopped at Crianlarich, in the brief interval while passengers made a dash for the refreshment room, they got to work on the fire. There was more of the hardest mountain climbing ahead of us. I stayed on the station platform until the guard was ready to wave us the 'right away'. While such strenuous fire-raking and cleaning operations were in progress a third man on the footplate would have been in the way.

When I was welcomed aboard the needle of the steam pressure gauge was still well below its rated maximum of 200 lb per sq. in. but the fireman, laughing now like his normal self, hung his jacket over the gauge as if to say 'forget that thing', while the driver opened out, to show the engine no mercy. The wind and the rain lashed us as we roared our way up that bleak mountainside. The driver with his teeth set and his eyes screwed up frequently looked out over the side of the cab into the very face of the storm, while his fireman stoked with precision and skill; and then suddenly, as if to belie any thoughts I might have had about poor steaming, the safety valves lifted and the boiler was blowing off. The driver looked across and laughed, opening the regulator still wider, and the fireman's face was wreathed in smiles; but still he did not take his jacket off the pressure gauge. *Lord of the Isles* indeed; shabby that engine may have looked externally, but now it was kicking those fearsome gradients from beneath the wheels with an almost contemptuous ease.

The low cloud and oncoming dusk had thrown a blanket over the most dramatic spectacle of the West Highland line, the well-nigh perfect volcanic cone of Ben Doran towering to 3523 ft, and precisely ahead as the train tops the summit point at the Perth–Argyll County March. But travelling in such drear wintry weather sometimes brings a sight that the holiday visitors who used to throng the Sunday excursion trains from Glasgow were never likely to see. Running cautiously downhill, we had made our way round the celebrated 'Horse-shoe Bend' and were coming on to a straighter stretch on the very flanks of Ben Doran itself, when ahead of us was a herd of red deer, some actually on the line itself. There must have been a dozen or more of them watched over by a big fellow with magnificent antlers. They scattered at the sound of our whistle though he, as the monarch of them all, was the last to leap nimbly over the fence on to the open moorland. It was not the least of the thrills on that stormy run back to Fort William.

By the time I made that journey all was changing in the locomotive department of the Scottish railways. Sir Nigel Gresley, the designer of the 'K4' class, had been dead many years, and Edward Thompson, his successor, who in so short a time had tried to overturn so much that had previously been traditional, had also gone. With nationalization E. D. Trask became the first Motive Power Superintendent of the newly formed Scottish Region, incorporating the former L M S activities with his previous command. Soon, not from the locomotive department, there were ominous rumours about cutting out redundant facilities and closing one-time competitive lines. The once debated 'K4' engine *Mac Cailin Mor* was the victim of one of Thompson's depredations. It was rebuilt as a two-cylinder engine of considerably reduced tractive power to form the prototype of the new standard L N E R Class 'K1'. I had a ride on it in 1950, and was not impressed. The train was double-headed with no more than a moderate load, but my main impression of the trip was of the harsh and uncomfortable riding. Travelling south from Fort William I had had enough of it by the time we got to Crianlarich, and retired to the comfort of the train.

It was in 1949 that a new morning train had

been put on which foreshadowed the curtailment of railway facilities in the Western Highlands. Running from Glasgow to Oban it used the former L N E R route as far as Crianlarich, and there transferred via the connecting junction to the L M S route. At the time it was explained that by so doing the total distance was shortened by 16 miles, but of course by this route the train service to the Oban line from such stations as Stirling, Callander and Balquidder was eliminated. Then, it was the only Glasgow–Oban train that used the West Highland line, and it was actually scheduled to run non-stop from Glasgow to Crianlarich. Engines of the 'B1' class 4–6–0 type were used, with a crew change at Crianlarich. It was the first regular use of engines of the 4–6–0 type on the West Highland, and with the gradual integration of L M S and L N E facilities after nationalization some engines of the Stanier 'Black Five' 4–6–0

Ex-North British Railway 'Glen' class 4–4–0, of a design introduced in 1913. The *Glen Dochart*, here seen at Eastfield shed, Glasgow, in 1950, was one of a batch built in 1919–20   *A. G. Ellis*

class were also introduced. These latter had been in regular use on the Callander and Oban line since 1939. Neither the 'B1' nor the 'Black Five' 4–6–0s improved the position so far as piloting was concerned on the West Highland. The nominal tractive power of both classes was considerably less than that of the Gresley 'K4' 2–6–0s and the maximum load they were permitted to take single-handed was 240 tons – not all that much greater than the 220 tons of the old 'K2' 2–6–0.

Nevertheless, in the last years of steam on the West Highland line the 4–6–0s, whether 'Black Fives' or 'B1s', took over almost completely on the original line between Glasgow and Fort William, and the working of the five remaining 'K4' 2–6–0s was concentrated on the Mallaig extension. The curvature west of Glenfinnan is very severe, and the longer wheelbase of the 4–6–0s did not take kindly to it. When I first travelled over that section of the line, in 1932, the entire regular traffic, passenger and goods alike, was being worked by those remarkably tough superheated North British 0–6–0s of the 'J37' class. They may not have been quite so easy on the curves as the passenger 4–4–0s of the 'Glen' class, but their greater adhesion was valuable on the very steep gradients. On the West Highland proper, south of Fort William, I found, from many detailed observations of train running, the 'Glens' quite unequalled for their tractive effort. The maximum rostered load for a single engine was 180 tons, and with that load they were consistently and markedly faster on the banks than a 'K2' with 220 tons, or a 'K4' with anything approaching the full 300 tons. The fastest of all my West Highland runs, in both directions, were made by a pair of 'Glens' with 350 tons between them.

In the last years of steam loads seemed to have diminished. With so many families having their own cars those Sunday excursions from Glasgow to Fort William no longer had the appeal they exercised in the 1930s, and while with trains within their maximum loads the 'Black Five' 4–6–0s could make light work of the gradients there was not the drama of hard slogging about a journey over the line as when a 'K2' or a 'K4' was really up against it. A 'Black Five' streaking up Glen Orchy at 45–50 mph with a five-coach train of 170 tons was rather akin to a modern HST doing 60 mph up the worst gradients of the Cornish main line, where 'Halls' and 'Castles' would be struggling to maintain 30 mph. This is not to say that

The 'K4' class 2–6–0 *Cameron of Lochiel*, when first built, painted passenger engine green and numbered 3443 on a southbound goods from Fort William to Glasgow, on the West Highland line at Crianlarich, in 1939
O. S. Nock

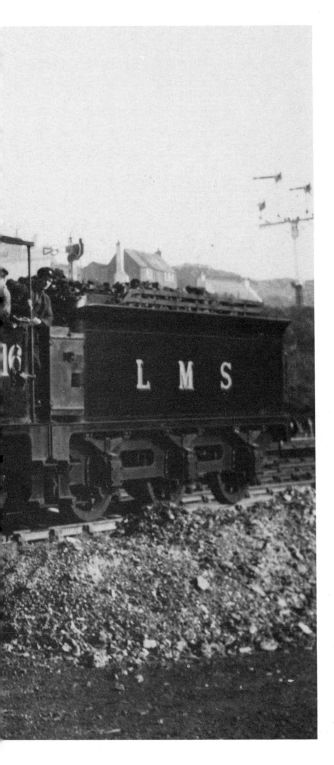

there were no great moments in the last years of steam on the West Highland line, but the highlights came on special occasions rather than in the ordinary run of traffic, and particularly when locomotives that would otherwise have been complete strangers visited the line.

One of the most unusual of these visitations came in the early summer of 1956. There was to be a great gathering of the Clan Cameron at Achnacarry, the ancestral home of Locheil, the chief of the Clan. Lochiel himself was at that time Chairman of the Area Board of Scottish Region of British Railways, and the idea was conceived of using the then relatively new 'B R 6' class 'Pacific' engine *Clan Cameron* to haul the special train from Glasgow to Spean Bridge, the nearest station on the line to Achnacarry. There had, of course, been a Highland 4–6–0 engine named *Clan Cameron*, which in its later years was working on the Oban line, but it had been withdrawn and scrapped some ten years earlier. The problem with the new *Clan Cameron* was its length, in relation to the incessant curvature of the line. The engine wheelbase was 35 ft 9 in. as compared to the 27 ft 2 in. of a 'Black Five', but so far as flexibility on the curves was concerned the rear radial track of the *Clan* would probably have made it sweeter riding than a 4–6–0; the main concern was with side clearances, because of the much greater length of the rigid main frames. However, the civil engineer gave his consent for a trial run and on 10 May the engine took the afternoon train from Glasgow up to Fort William, returning with the 9.31 a.m. up on the following morning. All was apparently well, and preparations went ahead for the special run on 16 June. As befitted so special a day for the Clan, the train crew was specially recruited and the driver, fireman and guard all had the surname Cameron. In case of any trouble occurring the operating department had the 'K4' 2–6–0 engine

In the rock-girt engine yard at Kyle of Lochalsh: the ex-Highland Railway 4–4–0 No. 14416 *Ben a'Bhuird*, of Peter Drummond's 'Small Ben' class   *O. S. Nock*

Cameron of Lochiel standing pilot at Crianlarich, but it was not needed.

After this special occasion the West Highland reverted to normal, though significantly on a downward scale of business activity. The 'Black Five' 4–6–0s continued on the Glasgow–Fort William section, with the 'K4' 2–6–0s on the Mallaig extension, but before the decade was ended, with steam locomotives being scrapped in all directions on British Railways, it was evident that the West Highland could not escape. From the locomotive point of view it was grouped with the Callander and Oban, and in 1960 the joint allocation was 45 steam units, mostly of the L M S 'Black Five' 4–6–0s; but it was then estimated that the work on the two routes taken together could be done by no more than 23 diesel–electrics of the Type 2 power category, aided by four diesel shunting loco-motives. The curtain was about to descend. The 'K4' 2–6–0s had been moved away to third-rate local duties; by the end of 1961 they had all been condemned, and it was only through a private purchaser that *The Great Marquess* was saved from the scrap heap. But in 1961 arrangements were made for a farewell run, and *Cameron of Lochiel* was rescued from humdrum duties in Fife and tuned up sufficiently to make a passenger run from Glasgow to Fort William.

To the delight of all those who had known the West Highland in its greatest days British Rail-ways decided to preserve one of the 'Glen' class 4–4–0 engines and restore it to its original North British Railway style and livery. This was No. 256 *Glen Douglas*. It needed no rebuilding in the generally acknowledged sense because the design, first introduced in 1913, had remained completely unchanged. The preserved engine was only the third of the class to be built at Cowlairs Works, and dating from September of that year was thus approaching 50 years of age at the time of her restoration. In the minds of railway enthusiasts who were not old enough to know the North British in pre-Grouping days there was always some doubt as to what the colour of the locomotives really was. In some colour plates published in journals prior to 1920 it was rendered as a rich brown, almost reaching the shade artists know as 'madder', while others who claimed to have known the railway described the engine colour as 'green'. I saw North British engines for the first time in 1923, after Grouping, and they were then shabby, none too clean, and obviously awaiting repainting in the new L N E R colours. They had a dirty yellow brown look. The true colour was bronze, which in certain lighting had a definite greenish hue, but it was superbly rendered on the restored *Glen Douglas*.

It was natural that this engine featured in several farewell runs over the line in 1963, sometimes in partnership with one of her splendid goods contemporaries of the 0–6–0 'J37' class. But in that same year two gaily adorned strangers came to the West Highland on trips organized by the railway enthusiast fraternity. Both were preserved relics, but in excellent working order. Naturally they were not expected to work as hard as the 'Glens' of old, but they brought a charming atmosphere to the line. One of these was the famous Caledonian 4–2–2 No. 123, decked in the ever-memorable blue livery. She was no stranger to the neighbouring Oban line, because in the far-off days of the Caledonian Railway she used occasionally to work through from Callander to Oban hauling an engineers' inspection saloon. On her old line, since restoration, she double-headed the *Glen Douglas* on special excursions to Oban. The other visitor to the West Highland was the former Great North of Scotland 4–4–0 *Gordon Highlander*, an extremely handsome little engine at any time, but elegant beyond measure in the splendour of the restored green livery – a colour quite different from the bronze of the North British *Glen Douglas*.

The last years of steam: the early 1960s proved more so for the West Highland than for many another line, which became re-invigorated with nostalgia once the ban on steam was lifted and charter trains could once again be organized. So far as the Scottish veterans were concerned it was felt by some that their day of active performance was done, and when an extension to the Glasgow Museum of Transport was planned, in 1966, *Glen Douglas*, the Caledonian 4–2–2 No. 123, and the *Gordon Highlander*, together with the very historic Jones Goods 4–6–0 of the Highland Railway were handed over to become no more than museum pieces, with their days of running presumably ended for ever. But one can never be sure where steam locomotives are concerned. For into that museum with them went a Caledonian standard 0–6–0 goods engine, and since then it has been extracted and transferred to Aviemore to work on the Speyside Railway.

CHAPTER
—11—

THE 'SETTLE AND CARLISLE'

In most respects this famous line could be regarded as the very epitome of a mountain railway. It abounds in fine structures, dramatically poised against the wild Pennine background; its tunnels, long and brilliantly surveyed in such a terrain, involved so many hardships and hazards in their construction that the toll in human life was considerable. The scenery needless to say is on the grandest north country scale, but in one respect the 'Settle and Carlisle' stands conspicuously alone among the mountain railways of the whole world. It is to all intents and purposes *straight*. There are curves, of course, but they are so superbly laid out that in its entire length from its junction with the 'Little North Western', 1½ miles south of Settle itself, to Petteril Bridge Junction, where on the outskirts of Carlisle it joins the Newcastle and Carlisle line of the former North Eastern Railway, there was not a single speed restriction in the greatest days of steam: 72 miles of superb railroad, where the Midland expresses of eighty years ago used occasionally to top 90 mph! Today if the traffic warranted it and finance was forthcoming there would be no difficulty in upgrading the line for 125 mph running throughout.

How was it that such a line was built through the mountains in the early 1870s? For in so rugged a countryside, and one including so many vicissitudes and freaks of geology, the cost – even for those days – was astronomical. It was because the Midland Railway Board, frustrated by a 'by your leave' arrangement in which they reached Carlisle and the tracks of their potential Scottish partners by running powers over a substantial length of the London and North Western Railway, resolved to have a line of their own, come what may. The distance by the Settle and Carlisle route would be about 24 miles longer from London to Carlisle than by the North Western, and to compete effectively for the Anglo-Scottish traffic there had to be no restrictions on speed in the north country other than the labour of climbing the gradients. That handicap was shared in full measure by the North Western in climbing over Shap, and although their summit level of 915 ft was more than 200 ft lower than that of the Midland at Aisgill Moor, their average speeds over the 69 miles from Lancaster to Carlisle were no better than those of the Midland over the 76 miles northward from Hellifield.

In the early days of railway literature little was written about the beauties of the passing scene, probably because relatively little of it could be seen from the compartment-style carriages of the day. In F. S. Williams's *History of the Midland Railway* there were some dramatic engravings, but one suspected that the features of the mountain landscape had been much exaggerated; and in a two-instalment article in *The Railway Magazine* in 1905 its pages were packed with naught but details of train services, and pictures of little but station buildings. Then in 1916 I was sent to board at Giggleswick School, and I saw the line for myself. I cannot begin to describe the intensity with which the atmosphere of that wonderful countryside gripped my imagination, and in the five years that I was there, having many opportunities for exploring the country and its unique natural features, those first boyhood impressions were consolidated and have remained vividly with me all my life. Nowhere else in the world have my railway interests and my love of wild mountain country been more thoroughly and happily integrated, and even in those sad days when the boffins of 222 Marylebone Road sought to obliterate all memories of steam traction, the unique appeal of the 'Settle and Carlisle' was if anything intensified when seen from a privileged seat in the cab of a diesel. But steam could not be kept quiet for ever, and the day came when this choicest of all north country routes was passed as one of those where steam specials would be permitted.

Unfortunately the reprieve came too late for the great celebrations of the centenary of the completion of the line, in 1976, and the anniversary trains had to be hauled over it by diesels – not very punctually as it turned out! At that time British Railways were just recovering from the days of Mr Shirley, one of whose principal aims seems to have been to destroy every vestige of sentiment, and indeed of physical reminder of the old steam railways, as though it had been an evil age of which every memory should be obliterated. Fortunately the depredations of his lackeys had not gone too far by the time he left for Australia, to cause similar distress on the New South Wales Railways; but the acceptance of steam specials in 1976 on British Railways was guarded, and ringed with objections that were more imaginary than real. A very strong plea was made, by persons of high influence, for the 'Settle and Carlisle' centenary specials to be hauled by steam; but the case foundered on the then seemingly insurmountable rock that the loco-motives would have to pass under the overhead electric wires at Carlisle, and that the risk of flash-over due to their exhausts could not be accepted.

The point was taken, but so significant was the occasion deemed that a fresh suggestion was made that the centenary special should be steam-hauled to Durran Hill Junction, where the North Eastern line from Newcastle was joined, and diesel-hauled over the last mile into Carlisle Citadel station. No, this could not be arranged either. Perhaps it was just as well after all, as things turned out, because there were no Midland engines available to haul the special. It was planned to originate at Carn-forth, and the best that could be done in the way of 'auld lang syne' was to work this train across country to Hellifield by the preserved Midland compound, No. 1000, and a Stanier 'Black Five' 4–6–0 that had regularly worked over the Settle and Carlisle line in days gone by. But when my wife and I arrived at Giggleswick on the eve of the trip we learned that both had failed. In great urgency the Gresley 'Pacific' *Flying Scotsman* was being moved across from York to Carnforth, while to provide some vintage flavour, albeit of an alien character for the occasion, the little L N W R 2–4–0 *Hardwicke*, which was already at Carnforth and in good running order, was to be used as pilot to the 'Pacific' on the run to Hellifield. The irony of it was that in little more than a year's time the ban on steam over the Settle and Carlisle line was lifted, and steam-hauled charter trains began to enter and leave Carlisle station.

The final dénouement, so far as British Railways and steam haulage on the Settle and Carlisle line was concerned, came in the winter of 1979–80 when the Marketing Manager of the London Midland Region, realizing that steam-hauled tour trains were good business, introduced the Cumbrian Mountain Express, a circular tour train running from Preston to Carlisle and back, in one direction electrically hauled over Shap and in the other over the Settle and Carlisle line, with steam-haulage between Carlisle and Skipton, and again from Skipton to Carnforth. The Cumbrian Mountain Express was run by British Railways, not as a charter tour train, and for the Carlisle–Skipton and Skipton–Carnforth stages B R had to hire steam locomotives from the Steam Locomotive Operators Association. It was significant of the confidence British Railways had come to place on the locomotives and back-up services of S L O A that they embarked on this highly appreciated new train service. By using a variety of loco-motives from three out of the four main-line rail-ways of pre-nationalization days, it was hoped that patrons would come again and again, which indeed many of them have done. It is unfortunate that structure-gauge clearances precluded the use of any ex-Great Western locomotives.

The use of Skipton as the exchange point between the north–south and east–west parts of the steam-hauled itinerary was not only logical in view of the general run-down of facilities at Helli-field and the convenience for patrons to join or leave the trains at that very pleasant north country town, but also interesting in that it revived memories of the earliest days of Anglo-Scottish working over the Settle and Carlisle line. When the age-old rivalry between the East and West Coast routes from London to Scotland began to warm up, first in 1888, to an undisguised com-petition in speed, and seven years later to the all-out race to the north, the Midland had to do something about it, even though they were not directly involved in the racing. Their route

The southern end of the line, Settle Junction showing the 'Little North Western' line to Carnforth to left, and a Glasgow–Leeds express hauled by a 'Britannia' 4–6–2 No. 70054 *Dornoch Firth*, coming down off the Settle and Carlisle line, in 1962

Derek Cross

Days of the Cumbrian Mountain Express: the 'Black Five' 4–6–0 with Stephenson's link motion, climbing hard near Helwith Bridge (February 1981)

David Eatwell

through the north country having by that time been fully consolidated, they retimed the morning Scotch express from St Pancras in 1888 to run throughout to Carlisle in separate portions for Glasgow and Edinburgh. This was before the days of corridor carriages and dining cars, and the Midland had hitherto made their luncheon stop at Normanton, where there was a palatial dining-room on the station platform, just as the West Coast made their luncheon stop at Preston and the East Coast at York. But with the Midland then having Scotch expresses leaving London at 10.30

a.m. for Glasgow and 10.40 a.m. for Edinburgh, it was not to be expected that Normanton could cope with two trains for lunch in rapid succession, with their half-hour stops overlapping in time; so it was arranged that the Edinburgh train should pass ahead of the Glasgow at Normanton, while passengers of the latter were lunching, and that the Edinburgh passengers should lunch in Leeds.

Meanwhile the Glasgow train, leaving Normanton soon after the Edinburgh had passed through, ran non-stop to Skipton, by-passing Leeds altogether by means of the Whitehall Junction avoiding line. And then, changing engines (for which the modest allowance of three minutes was made in the timetable), it ran non-stop to Carlisle. In that era Skipton was an important locomotive depot on the Midland Railway. Several times recently, when the Cumbrian Mountain Express has arrived from Carnforth and the fresh engine for the run to Carlisle has been attached at what had been the rear end, I have tried to picture what it must have been like in 1888 when the Midland with the 7-ft 2–4–0 engines of the '101' class were changing engines in three minutes, or as near to it as they could manage. Four of those beautiful little engines, introduced by S. W. Johnson in 1877, were at Skipton for many years. When dining-cars

were introduced on the Midland Scotch expresses and the Normanton luncheon stop became unnecessary, the morning Glasgow express from St Pancras still avoided Leeds, and the only passenger stop between Leicester and Skipton was at Chesterfield. The abolition of the luncheon stop made possible an acceleration of 16 minutes between St Pancras and Carlisle, as illustrated in Table 7. It will be seen that in the later timetable one minute extra was allowed for changing engines at Leicester and Skipton. The train of 1899 ran the 86¾ miles from Skipton to Carlisle in 108 minutes, an average speed of 48 mph.

In 1901 however the Anglo-Scottish service by the Midland route was reorganized, and timed to

Memories of past grandeur: a Kirtley '800' class 2–4–0, many of which worked on the Settle and Carlisle, photographed outside St Pancras

British Railways

Table 7

Midland Railway: 10.30 a.m. London to Glasgow

Distance (miles)			Year 1888	Year 1899
—	St Pancras	dep.	10.30	10.30
99¼	Leicester	arr.	12.25	12.25
		dep.	12.29	12.30
146¼	Chesterfield	arr.	—	1.32
		dep.	—	1.35
185¼	Normanton	arr.	2.13	—
		dep.	2.38	—
221¼	Skipton	arr.	3.24	3.08
		dep.	3.27	3.12
308	Carlisle	arr.	5.16	5.00

make it more directly competitive with its East Coast and West Coast rivals. More particularly, so far as the Settle and Carlisle was concerned, the new 9.30 a.m. and 1.30 p.m. expresses from St Pancras were timed to pass through Carlisle just ahead of the 10 a.m. and 2 p.m. expresses from Euston. This was no mean feat, having regard to the greater mileage and the complexities of the Midland route between Trent and Leeds. One effect of the change, however, was that in future Skipton would no longer be a stopping station, let alone an engine-changing point. While one would have thought that the Midland had a large potential Scottish traffic from the many large towns lying on or near to its main route, statistics taken in the early 1900s showed that 78 per cent of the clientele of the so-designated 'Scotch Expresses' – Scotch, be it noted, not Scots or Scottish! – originated at St Pancras. This was enough to justify the omission of all stops other than those essential for locomotive purposes. It was interesting to see in the public timetables, as evidenced by the copy reproduced here that the scenic attractions of the Settle and Carlisle routes were emphasized.

This does not relate to the last years of steam, but it is important in showing that whatever the

---

JULY NOTICES, 1901.

Revised and improved Express Service
BETWEEN

ENGLAND AND SCOTLAND

BY THE MOST INTERESTING ROUTE, Via SETTLE AND CARLISLE.

Through the Lovely Valleys of the Ribble and the Eden,
By the Home and Haunts of Sir Walter Scott,
The Land of Robert Burns, the Forth Bridge, &c.

From JULY 1st the following improved Service will come into operation:—

TO SCOTLAND. WEEKDAYS.

	LONDON (St Pancras)	LEICESTER	NOTTINGHAM	BRISTOL	BIRMINGHAM	DERBY	SHEFFIELD	LEEDS	BRADFORD	LIVERPOOL (Exchange)	MANCHESTER (Victoria)	CARLISLE	GLASGOW	GREENOCK	EDINBURGH	OBAN	FORT WILLIAM	MALLAIG	PERTH	ABERDEEN	INVERNESS

[Dense reproduced timetable of express times to Scotland.]

FROM SCOTLAND. WEEKDAYS.

	INVERNESS	ABERDEEN	PERTH	MALLAIG	FORT WILLIAM	OBAN	EDINBURGH	GREENOCK	GLASGOW	CARLISLE	MANCHESTER (Victoria)	LIVERPOOL (Exchange)	BRADFORD	LEEDS	SHEFFIELD	DERBY	BIRMINGHAM	BRISTOL	NOTTINGHAM	LEICESTER	LONDON (St Pancras)

[Dense reproduced timetable of express times from Scotland.]

A—Via Chesterfield. B—Via Leeds. C—From July 23rd inclusive only. D—Monday mornings excepted. E—From September 2nd to 10th only. F—From Leicester and Nottingham commencing July 15th. G—Via Trent. H—6.0 p.m. on Saturdays. J—Bank Holidays excepted.
K—Will apply until August 31st only. L—Sundays excepted. M—Saturdays excepted.

FOR COMPLETE TIME TABLE OF SCOTCH CONNECTIONS AND SUNDAY SERVICES, SEE PAGES 130 TO 133.

NOTE.—The Thin Line between the Hour and Minute Figures indicates p.m.

---

statistically minded railway *littérateurs* of eighty years ago might think, its owners felt sure they held a trump card in the scenic attractions of the Settle and Carlisle line. There is, indeed, no doubt that in pre-Grouping days many travellers from London to both Edinburgh and Glasgow preferred the Midland route. Despite that popularity it was very many years before it spread to what may be called the lineside sector of railway enthusiasts. Until the curtain descended upon the pleasure of photographing trains at speed, in September 1939, I can think of no more than three or four occasions when photographs on the Settle and Carlisle line had appeared in *The Railway Magazine*, as compared to countless examples on the line over Shap. In days when railway enthusiasts who also owned cars were few and far between, the choicest scenic localities were relatively inaccessible, and the train service to stations like Dent, Hawes Junction (later Garsdale) and Kirkby Stephen sparse indeed. It was not until after the end of the Second World War that my late friends Bishop Eric Treacy and Maurice Earley began to penetrate those north country fastnesses.

The days when railway enthusiast groups seemed to have eyes and ears for all that was going on, or about to go on, had not yet arrived. Not yet had come the day when a harassed senior locomotive officer could exclaim, 'If I want to know what is going on in my works I have to read the

A broadside view of the preserved 4–6–2 No. 46229 *Duchess of Hamilton* crossing the Ribble at Helwith Bridge, with the Cumbrian Mountain Express, November 1980   *David Eatwell*

"XYZ" magazine . . .', the journal of one of the most erudite enthusiast societies. In 1923 no one on the L M S had thought to inform the railway world that a most exciting series of competitive dynamometer car engine trials was about to begin between Carlisle and Leeds, in which engines of the former Midland, London and North Western, and Caledonian Railways were going to be involved; or even after nationalization that scientifically regulated trials of unprecedented severity were being conducted from time to time. It is true that in due course technical details of these trials were published, but for every enthusiast interested in details of power output, coal consumption and such-like there were scores who would have travelled untold miles to photograph these engines in full action, and record the thrilling sounds of them on tape.

Fascinating and technically valuable as were the data secured in these Brobdingnagian trials of strength on the long gradients leading up to Aisgill from the north and Blea Moor from the south, the commercial usefulness of it all was soon to be nullified when in 1955 British Railways decided to make an end of steam traction. From the viewpoint of historical record it is rather tragic that a series of trials representing the ultimate in performance for a number of famous steam locomotive types should have been almost completely unrecorded photographically, save for a few snaps taken as opportunity presented itself by individual members of the testing staff. The approximate dates at which these test runs were made were:

June 1951	'Britannia' class No. 70005 *John Milton*
August 1951	ex-L N E class 'B1' 4–6–0 No. 61353
March 1952	B R class '5' 4–6–0 No. 73008
Autumn 1952	'Merchant Navy' class 4–6–2
1953	Check trials on 'Britannia' No. 70025
1956	ex-L M S 4–6–2 No. 46225 *Duchess of Gloucester*

The B R trials were all conducted on special trains, and they were run between Carlisle and Skipton in each case to avoid the inconvenience of working the lengthy test trains into and out of Leeds. The L M S trials from 1923 onwards were made on ordinary service trains, to which the dynamometer car was attached between the tender and the train.

What the 'scrap-steam' disciples of Mr Shirley fondly hoped would be the very last steam train ever to run on British Railways was a 'special' from Liverpool to Carlisle and back, via Manchester, Blackburn, Hellifield and Settle, on 11 August 1968. Never previously had so many photographs been taken of a single train on this most cherished of English main lines. That this 'farewell' train has happily proved to be very far from the last was shown remarkably soon after, and one can turn back wistfully to the pages of *The Railway Magazine* for October of that year and experience again the interest and the nostalgic delight that the trip created. And now, after the triumphant return of steam, and the joy of photographing and riding in the Cumbrian Mountain Express, there is the very real fear that the Settle and Carlisle line may have to be closed altogether, not because of any anti-steam bias, not because of horrific documents like the Serpell Report, but because the revenue derived from the line and its ever-present value as a relief route to Shap are not likely to be sufficient to defray the cost of the repairs that are becoming necessary to the greatest of all its engineering structures, Ribblehead viaduct.

No one can now complain, however, that it has not been fully documented photographically. The most expert workers in the earliest days of moving train photography concentrated almost their entire attention on the train itself, securing sharpness of definition with cameras having focal plane

---

The southbound Cumbrian Mountain Express photographed from above the north portal of Blea Moor Tunnel, and hauled by ex-Southern 4–6–0 No. 850 *Lord Nelson* in July 1980   *David Eatwell*

shutters, at the expense of distortion of the locomotive. While some used apparatus that yielded
this distortion longitudinally, others devised
apparatus that rendered it vertically. I do not
know which was worse! But with modern
apparatus and ultra-rapid film not only is distortion eliminated but the photographers themselves

Coasting downhill past the now closed Stainforth
quarries the preserved *Sir Nigel Gresley* at the head
of the southbound Cumbrian Mountain Express in
July 1981

David Eatwell

are vying with one another in the sheer artistry of their work. As a boy I came to know the line between Settle Junction and Blea Moor intimately, though unfortunately with little or no opportunity for photography, and it has been a delight to me to see how all the well-remembered viewpoints have been captured by present-day photographers, in so many varieties of aspect, and all producing pictures that evoke the wonderful north country atmosphere of the line. Certainly the photographers of today have some rich and varied railway material on which to work, in the diversity and colour of the preserved locomotives, and in the invariable magnificence of their turn-out.

Inevitably those of us with very long memories grow rather wistful at the thought of the opportunities that were let slip in the early years of the present century, when the turn-out of Midland locomotives was at the very height of splendour, when the goods engines were burnished as lovingly as any of the others and a photographer waiting beneath the slopes of Wild Boar Fell or at Helwith Bridge might have the luck to 'cop' one of the earliest of the three-cylinder compounds, with its huge bogie tender. It is true that to the uninitiated there was a sameness about Midland trains, in that everything was red, engines and carriages alike. But what a red that deep lustrous colour was! Think of such spacious and prosperous days that time could be spared to give the carriages seventeen coats of paint, and for the company to pay a five per cent dividend on its ordinary shares. The engines were no less splendidly finished, though the amount of polished brasswork was always kept discreetly restrained. But those highly polished Midland engines never seemed to get photographed against the glorious countryside of the Settle and Carlisle line; it was usually against some factory wall or the gasometers outside St Pancras! It must not be forgotten, however, that when the Settle and Carlisle line was first opened in 1876, Midland engines were painted green. In earlier days it had been a rather dark colour, but in his new 2–4–0 express engines spe-cially introduced for the Scotch traffic over the new line Mr S. W. Johnson adopted a much lighter green, of a pleasing shade that can be appreciated from one of the exhibits in the remarkable and comprehensive working model in the Derby Museum and Art Gallery. In 1913 *The Locomotive Magazine* had a colour plate showing one of these engines.

I am glad that some of our expert present-day photographers are using the attractive river crossing at Helwith Bridge as a setting for some of their pictures, and seeing *Lord Nelson*, *Leander* or *Sir Nigel Gresley* in this location takes me back to a time when I was still at Giggleswick. An extra half-holiday had been granted for some reason that I can't remember, and a school friend and I were making a cycling round trip to Austwick and back, outward via the Kendal road then across the moors and back through the Stainforth gorge. Just as we approached Helwith Bridge the signals were pulled off for an up train, and we waited to see what would come. It was a cloudless day in early spring, and the sinking sun was turning the browns of the moorland into a warm russet, when far up the line towards Horton we spotted the oncoming train – an express travelling fast. On the steep descending gradient she was running practically without steam, but what a picture she made, in the perfect harmony of engine and carriages glistening in the sunlight, all polished fit for a Royal Train. The engine was a Class '3' 4–4–0 and the carriages, not many of them, were all uniformly clerestory roofed. Against the glowing brown moorland that crimson lake engine and train made an unforgettable picture. It was not often that we enjoyed such benign weather in those regions.

Overlooking the great Ribblehead viaduct, whose fate and indeed that of the line itself now lies in the balance, is the finest of all English mountains, Ingleborough, so poised in compara-tive isolation from the rest of the Pennines as to be a prominent object even from as far afield as Morecambe Bay. Many who have never read *The Heart of Midlothian* will be familiar with the description of it from Jeanie Deans, Scott's tender-hearted heroine who trudged barefoot for much of the way from Edinburgh to London to plead the case of her sister imprisoned in the Old Tolbooth for a crime she had not committed. Walking on, south of Newark, and advised that Gonerby Hill lay ahead of her, she rejoiced for she found the level country ' . . . very wearisome to my Scotch een. When I lost sight of a muckle blue hill they ca' Ingleboro', I thought I hadna a friend left in this strange land.' But she could not have seen it so dramatically as it is presented to anyone riding south on the footplate. The moment the engine emerges from the dank, smoke-laden interior of Blea Moor tunnel there, directly ahead, is Ingleborough in all its majesty towering up to 2373 ft. Familiarity with the scene has never diminished the thrill with which I look out for it every time I travel that way.

One memory is of the summit itself, broad and flat enough – as a party of us once found – for an impromptu game of stump-cricket; and another is of emergence from the tunnel on a dismal November afternoon when the drizzling rain, mixed with sleet, had made the rail conditions very bad and, with a near-maximum load, a little time had been lost climbing to Aisgill. It was in the days when the North Western 'Claughton' class 4–6–0s had replaced the Midland compounds as the premier passenger engines north of Leeds. It was also unfortunately before the days when I had the privilege of an engine-pass, because I would dearly have liked to be in the cab that day. We left Blea Moor tunnel at a shade below 60 mph and once on to the descending gradient the acceleration was uncanny: the sidings and goods loops, only a mile from the tunnel, were passed at 70 mph; 78 mph over the great viaduct, and before Horton-in-Ribblesdale we were doing 88 mph and still accelerating. With early nightfall adding to the undoubted difficulty in sighting signals on that afternoon of mist and sleet, however, the driver eased up a little nearing Helwith Bridge and we crossed the well-remembered bridge at no more than 67 mph, but we were soon into the seventies once again, and rounded off our spell on the famous line with a rousing 77½ mph past Settle Junction.

No such speeds are now permitted over the Settle and Carlisle line. Not even in its palmiest days could it have been described as an intensively used route, and in order to lessen the amount of track maintenance the maximum speed throughout has been limited to 60 mph. So that whatever the distinguished preserved locomotives might have been able to do in their prime they nowadays have to drift downhill without steam on the Cumbrian Mountain Express. As to maximum speed I am not likely to forget what happened on the 'Three Summits Tour' train organized by the Railway Correspondence and Travel Society on Sunday, 30 June 1963. The three summits were Aisgill, Beattock and Shap, to be surmounted in the course of a round trip from Leeds. On the first leg of the journey the ex-L N E R 'A4' Pacific *Golden Eagle* had injector trouble. Indeed, during the stop at Skipton there was talk of replacing her – horror of horrors! – with a diesel. But the trouble was rectified sufficiently for us to start away again, though, with only one injector working, the ascent of the 'Long Drag' from Settle Junction up to Blea Moor could not be made as vigorously as those on the footplate wished. The best that could be done, with a load of no more than 360 tons, was 33–5 mph. Once over Aisgill summit however and a satisfactory level of water in the boiler established, *Golden Eagle* was taken down to Carlisle like the proverbial bomb. We did not begin to make any *real* speed until after Kirkby Stephen, but then over the 34.4 miles from Crosby Garrett to Cumwhinton we averaged 81 mph. We reached a full 90 mph at Ormside viaduct, rushed the rise to Appleby at 82 mph, and stormed over the next 15.6 miles to Lazonby at an average of 85 mph – thrilling memories indeed!

Winter sunshine above the Eden gorge near Armathwaite, as the three-cylinder 4–6–0 No. 5690 *Leander* passes with the southbound Cumbrian Mountain Pullman in January 1982   *David Eatwell*

The photographers of today have certainly made the most of their scenic opportunities on the beautiful stretch in the lower Eden valley between Lazonby and Armathwaite. In the early 1900s some apparently official photographs were taken by the Midland Railway in this neighbourhood, but the photographer in question did not venture far beyond the northern end of the Armathwaite down platform; and his pictures, while showing the variety of motive power then in use on the line, gave not the slightest impression of the scenic beauties that lay to the south of the station. It was left to my great friend the late Bishop Eric Treacy to explore, and then magnificently record on film, the sheer poetry of express train running in that area. Others have followed nobly in his footsteps.

Another stretch of the line that might have been in the Sahara for all the attention it had from photographers was that between Garsdale and the north end of Blea Moor tunnel. In the middle of the Second World War I had to go to Sheffield on engineering business, and one evening I was able to meet in person an enthusiast who had been a pen-friend for some time previously, C. M. Doncaster. He was a much older man than I, and had a collection of solo-locomotive photographs going back to the turn of the century. In later years he had been content with occasional snaps with a quite unsophisticated apparatus, but his collection was fascinating in its diversity, and one that he showed me on that occasion pulled me up with a jerk. It was a high-level view of Denthead viaduct lying just to the north end of Blea Moor tunnel, taken from the road straggling down the steep hillside. It was the first I had ever seen in that locality, and although the passing train in the picture was nothing more glamorous than a Mid-

A Midland 2–4–0, now preserved, the chassis, wheels and machinery of which are older than the Settle and Carlisle railway itself. The works plate bears the inscription 'Built Derby 1866'. This beautiful little engine is now preserved at the Midland Railway centre at Butterley, Derbyshire   *British Railways*

land '4F' 0–6–0 on a mixed goods, going north, the picture gripped my imagination, and he gave me a print. I painted the scene in watercolour, though substituting for the actual goods train a Johnson compound and a train of eight Clayton clerestories speeding south.

Since that time many others have found that wonderful stretch of line and the names Arten Gill, Dent and Rise Hill Tunnel are household words among those who travel in the charter specials, or focus their cameras on the Cumbrian Mountain Express. Now one has the strange situation that the remaining regular through passenger trains have been diverted, and so also some of the heaviest freights; but that steam on the various specials has outlasted the big diesels is a cause for anxiety rather than rejoicing, because one cannot tell how long it will be before the curtain finally descends and the far-famed Settle and Carlisle line joins the ranks of those that are no more than memories. It will be tragic indeed if this should occur, because in so many ways it is a part of our national heritage: a monument to 19th-century industrial enterprise and consummate engineering skill, and a parade ground and demonstration track for some of the greatest feats of locomotive performance that Great Britain has ever seen.

INDEX